ARCHITECTURE IN EXISTING FABRIC
Planning   Design   Building

Johannes Cramer

Stefan Breitling

ARCHITECTURE IN EXISTING FABRIC
Planning Design Building

Birkhäuser

Basel • Boston • Berlin

Design and production: Atelier Fischer, Berlin
Translation: Julian Reisenberger, Weimar
Copyediting of the English edition: Caroline Behlen, Berlin

Lithography and printing: Ruksaldruck, Berlin
Binding: Kunst- und Verlagsbuchbinderei, Leipzig

This book is also available in a German edition:
ISBN 978-3-7643-7751-9

Bibliographic information published by The German National Library
The Deutsche Nationalbibliothek lists this publication in the Deutsche
Nationalbibliografie; detailed bibliographic data are available in the
Internet at http://dnb.ddb.de.

Library of Congress Control Number. 2007925788

This work is subject to copyright. All rights are reserved, whether the whole or part of the
material is concerned, specifically the rights of translation, reprinting, re-use of illustrations,
recitation, broadcasting, reproduction on microfilms or in other ways, and storage in data
banks. For any kind of use, permission of the copyright owner must be obtained.

© 2007 Birkhäuser Verlag AG
Basel • Boston • Berlin
P.O.Box 133, CH-4010 Basel, Switzerland
Part of Springer Science+Business Media
Printed on acid-free paper produced from chlorine-free pulp. TCF ∞
Printed in Germany

ISBN 978-3-7643-7752-6

9 8 7 6 5 4 3 2 1
www.birkhauser.ch

CONTENTS

9 **Architecture and the existing fabric**

15 **Architecture and time**
18 The built environment and identity
20 Old and new
24 The value of the built environment

29 **The planning process**
29 SPECIAL FEATURES OF THE PLANNING PROCESS
29 Protective measures and essential repairs
31 Preparatory investigations
31 The level of planning detail
  33 Casa de las Conchas, Salamanca, Spain
34 THE PARTICIPANTS
34 The client
35 The architect
35 The planning authorities
  37 Overview: Planning permission procedure
  41 Naumburg City Museum, Germany
42 The contractors
42 DECISION-MAKING AND COMMUNICATION

45 **Preparatory investigations**
47 RECORDING HISTORIC BUILDINGS
47 Property and geographic details
48 Documentary evidence and archives
50 Recording the building as found
54 Metric building survey
  59 Overview: Precision levels in measured surveys
66 BUILDING SURVEY
  67 Houses on the Mühlenstrasse, Havelberg, Germany
68 Building archaeology
  71 Nidaros Cathedral, Trondheim, Norway
  74 Heubach Castle, Germany
  75 Balbarini townhouse, Pisa, Italy
  78 Bernhard chapel, Owen, Germany
  79 Schminke house, Löbau, Germany

83 Structural survey

86 Technical and material investigations

89 Evaluation and interpretation – strengths and weaknesses

95 **Design strategies**

97 Designing with history

101 Disposition

102 Definition of appropriate function

103 Municipal archives in the Church of San Agostin, Valladolid, Spain

104 Sensitive interventions

105 Tabourettli Theatre in the old Spalenhof, Basel, Switzerland

107 Auxiliary constructions

109 Bank in a 19th century building, Budapest, Hungary

111 Design strategies

111 Corrective maintenance

112 Private residence, Venice, Italy

113 Medieval house, Bamberg, Germany

115 Modernisation

116 Palazzo as museum, Venice, Italy

119 Adaptation

121 Loft in an industrial building, Madrid, Spain

122 Conversion and extension of an industrial building, Göttelborn, Germany

125 Hotel in a monastery church, Maastricht, Netherlands

128 Tyrolean Museum of History, Tyrol Castle, Italy

130 Single family houses, Utrecht, Netherlands

131 Historic office building, Zurich, Switzerland

134 Replacement

137 Architectonic expression

137 Correspondence

139 Swimming pool, Spexhall Manor, Great Britain

140 German Federal Foreign Office, Berlin, Germany

141 Unification

143 Fragmentation

149 Town hall conversion and extension, Utrecht, Netherlands

150 Nuevos Ministerios, Madrid, Spain

151 Junction and delineation

154 British Museum, Queen Elizabeth II Great Court, London, Great Britain

156 Documentation centre of the former Nazi party rally ground, Germany

159 Detail planning

159 Prerequisites

159 Development not demolition

160 An element-for-element approach

162 Library, Eichstätt, Germany

163 Planning on the basis of an accurate measured survey

165 Principles

165 Repair not renew

167 A cumulative process

169 Naumburg City Museum, Germany

171 Reclaimed materials

175 Solutions: two examples

175 Upgrading the thermal performance of windows

176 Villa, Buchschlag, Germany

178 Repairing timber roof structures

183 Building works

183 Site facilities

185 The workshop principle

185 Protective measures for building elements on site

187 Heubach Castle, library and museum, Heubach, Germany

189 Supervising building works

191 Samples, tests and mock-ups

192 Specifications and quantities

194 Construction time and Costing

196 Scheduling works

196 Architect's fees

199 Sustainability

200 Facility Management

202 Monitoring and maintenance

203 Preserving property value

205 Appendix

207 Bibliography

213 Index of architects

215 Subject index

219 Illustration credits

221 On the authors

ARCHITECTURE AND THE EXISTING FABRIC

*It is a rare occurrence for a great building to be completed by the same person who began it.**

Leon Battista Alberti

The shrinking of many European cities at the end of the second millennium is a clear sign that the design and construction of new buildings is in steady decline. At the same time the alteration of existing built structures is becoming increasingly important. Society is growing more aware of ecological issues and the thoughtless demolition of old buildings is now perceived not only as an ecological waste but also as the eradication of local identity, of cultural heritage and of socio-economic values. Various studies estimate that between 50% and 70% of all construction work and about half of the entire economic volume of construction now concerns work on existing buildings. Yet, many architects are not adequately prepared for this shift in the focus of architectural work.

Up until well into the 20th century, architects have enjoyed a balance between the design of new buildings and designs for existing built structures, both tasks being regarded as of equal status. Michelangelo Buonarroti's brilliant plans for St. Peter's in Rome were informed by a number of constraints from the existing site as well as by the surrounding structures built by his predecessors. Almost all great architects up to the time of Karl Friedrich Schinkel have split their attention between new constructions and a commitment to architecture within existing built contexts. Only from the 1920s onwards conversion or modernisation work was discredited with terms like "conversion architect" or "building in existing fabric". Today, many architects find even the very suggestion that their design should be informed by what already exists so restrictive that they feel impossibly constrained in their creative liberty. This irrational fear is reinforced when the structure in question is a listed building. Listed buildings constitute perhaps 3% of the existing building stock, but the methods developed for their conservation and restoration have also proven applicable to more everyday existing buildings. Just as irrational is the belief that conservationists wish to hinder good modern architecture. There is no good reason for any of these reservations.

The suggestion that designs for existing built structures allow no room for creativity is also unfounded. A handful of famous architects from the 1960s

*Maxima quaeque aedificatio vix nunquam dabitur per eundem absolvi possit, qui posuerit.

The beginnings of consistent architectural design in existing building fabric: the conversion of the Castelvecchio in Verona, Italy, to a museum by Carlo Scarpa (1964).

have ably demonstrated the opposite, among them Carlo Scarpa, Karljosef Schattner, Aurelio Galfetti or Massimo Carmassi. Their projects clearly show exactly how exciting a task the qualitative development of existing buildings can be in the hands of an ambitious designer. For example, in the monograph of Herzog & de Meuron's work, more than a third are conversion projects for existing buildings.

The pioneers of the 1960s, embracing the innovative credo of the times, gave little consideration to the conservation of existing building fabric and resources. Today more attention is paid to these aspects. Many projects by prominent architects have proven that it is possible to unite diverse considerations in a qualitative design. The plans by David Chipperfield and Julian Harrap for the Neues Museum in Berlin are just one such example. Without compromising their design or aesthetic aspirations, they have been able to combine the existing building fabric, methodically recorded and analysed, with a modern concept to create a stimulating and yet restrained project. Such designs, founded both on methodical analysis and creativity, demonstrate the validity of this approach and should serve as examples for other architects.

All the above designers were, and are, aware that the design approach for new buildings is not always appropriate when developing designs for existing built structures. In addition to adhering to general building and planning regulations and fulfilling technical requirements, it is also necessary to consider the given condition and configuration of an existing building, as passed on to us by our predecessors, and the need and wish to integrate this into a future design. In order to achieve this, it is vital to obtain a clear picture of the initial condition. Accordingly, the methodical recording and surveying of the existing building is the first step in the planning process. Although often complex and laborious, these steps prove their worth further down the line. Without an understanding of the structural system, one cannot consider its characteristics; without knowledge of the historic value of the building, one risks damaging or destroying it in the design. A good understanding of the existing building allows one to intelligently take into account distortions and to bring out the qualities of the building materials as well as the building's artistic and historic value. It is therefore inevitable that designs for existing buildings will have to react to more complex parameters than a design for a new building. Consequently, the coordination requirements and negotiations are more complex. At times this may

The deliberately modern insertions to a restaurant in Hamburg, Germany, give the room an entirely new character (Jordan Mozer, 2005).

appear excessive and the architect may wish to discharge himself of this task. The architect is, however, better advised to grasp this as a challenge and to use it as a productive instrument for the design process.

Unfortunately, all too many building sites testify to the designer's unwillingness to engage with the existing situation: the building is reduced to its shell or outside walls and what results is then invariably more visual effect than a well-designed and constructive solution. In some cases, designers become overly enamoured with a fragment at the cost of the overall concept. Even the terminology employed is unclear: care, maintenance, renovation, refurbishment, conservation, restoration, repair, renewal, modernisation, replacement, reconstruction; the list goes on. Ill-defined terminology compounds the problem and it is no surprise that it leads to Babylonian confusion.

Against this background, this book aims to achieve three things: for those for whom this is their first foray into this field, the book clarifies the differences between planning new buildings and developing designs for existing built structures. This includes not only the greater degree of initial investigation necessary but also a shift in approach to design and planning. Secondly, for those who are primarily interested in design, the book describes and analyses different design approaches for relating new architecture to the existing built fabric, as they have become evident in the past. It should be clear that the discursive approach of the book does not intend to provide step-by-step instructions. And thirdly, the book details the particularities of construction sites in and around existing buildings.

Our main aim is to provide orientation, make connections and explain approaches. Although we have attempted to describe the wide range and variety of aspects as fully as possible, we cannot provide a conclusive overview. For this and other reasons, this book cannot serve as a manual for construction practice or as a handbook for solving practical design problems. Likewise, although we are much indebted to the topic and the many parallels it has to offer, this book is not a guideline for conservation practice. Others before us have provided instructive literature on this and we gladly refer to their work in each chapter.

There are important reasons for the architect and designer to examine and consider not only existing buildings in detail but also their own relationship to the values, qualities and constraints the buildings hold within them. The architect has to deal with complex interrelationships and juggle a variety of design parameters. There are at times many opportunities for things to go wrong, and a good result is therefore all the more satisfying. All those who embark with commitment on a design project for an existing building will discover a many-faceted and fascinating field of activity, one that is no less interesting than designing new buildings and one whose particular complexities present further interesting challenges. The historic building fabric contains not only a wealth of resources and undiscovered qualities but also no shortage of problems and defects which the architect will have to consider and work with. Respect and creativity, the ability to work in a team, to understand and coordinate very different kinds of information and not least personal expression will be needed. And when all is complete, the result will hopefully exhibit clarity and consistency and at the same time resist being one-dimensional. That is what makes good architecture. Those who in their design are able to respect the past, the present and the future, and to achieve a balance between cultural tradition, practical requirements and contemporary expression, will be contributing to the fundamental values of European society.

We would like to thank numerous owners and photographers for their help in providing us with extensive image material. Stimulating discussions with friends and colleagues have helped us clarify many aspects. Wolfgang Wolters aided us with advice and criticism. Thomas Eißing, Andreas Potthoff, Jens Birnbaum, Arne Semmler and Friedrich Schmidt produced illustrations for the book.

The complex and time-consuming picture editing would not have been possible without Anke Blümel's knowledgeable and committed input. Bernd Fischer's care and attention at both macro and micro level has given the book its beautiful form. We would finally like to thank both our publisher Birkhäuser and the editor Andreas Müller for their initiative and constructive assistance, without which the book would not have come to pass.

Johannes Cramer   Stefan Breitling

ARCHITECTURE AND TIME

The faster the future becomes the new, the unknown, the more continuity and past we must take with us into the future.* Odo Marquard

Architecture is always connected with time. Buildings are created out of specific circumstances, they are designed to fulfil a particular purpose, and their material and form are determined by the available means, techniques and traditions. Once completed, they are invariably subject to a variety of later transformations. A proverb reminds us that "the moment the last craftsman has left a house is the moment decay begins". The process of aging leaves traces. Surfaces acquire a patina which, depending on the aging properties of the material, can be protective, destructive as well as awe-inspiring. Constructions and joints loosen as part of the natural aging process, or are affected by outside influences such as fire or alterations. But more often, it is functional requirements and the needs and wishes of the owner and user that result in changes being made to existing buildings. Building constructions are not made to last forever.

In an analogy with human existence, the built environment demonstrates the delicate coexistence of longevity, gradual aging and sudden destruction. That these changes can occur in a time span of only a few years or after several hundred years is what makes architecture so fascinating. The traces and scars of history leave their mark on the building fabric in successive layers, becoming apparent at faults and joints. They are an inseparable part of a building and its qualities. The building fabric testifies not only to the moment of its creation and the intentions and possibilities of its creators, but also to history itself, the passage of time and the events and developments the building witnesses.

CHANGE is a natural condition of life. In addition to the natural process of aging, which architecture is also subject to, the changes made by the respective users play a particular role in the continued life of a building.

The quick succession of different historic circumstances, of fashions and styles and the rapid development of new building techniques have brought about the replacement of the old with the new throughout all ages of European history. The demolition of incomplete building works, the neglect of existing buildings and the removal of parts of them or their destruction

*Je schneller die Zukunft für uns das Neue, das Fremde wird, desto mehr Kontinuität und Vergangenheit müssen wir in die Zukunft nehmen.

Fractal architecture as a mirror of reality.

History produces layers. The façade of Barco Cornaro near Vicenza, Italy, with its wall paintings from the Renaissance has been modified repeatedly without regard for its historic beauty. One would take a different approach today.

can be seen wherever one looks. Change entails confronting the unknown, heralded in by the new, and calls what is known and familiar into question. Change can be unsettling, in particular when it is rapid and sudden and its irreversibility becomes painfully apparent. Yet, despite this, change is a constituent element of European culture.

Preservation is no contradiction to change. The architectural means with which one protects building substance and maintains its value through completion, renovation, reinforcement, conversion and extension of existing buildings also represents a modification of the pre-existing and thus is also a form of change. The maintenance and repair of one's own property with the aim of prolonging its lifetime and maintaining and improving its value has been a matter of course throughout the centuries. The ability to analyse a damaged building and develop appropriate and economic measures for its repair was particularly highly regarded as the mathematical consideration of statics gained increasing importance. Franz Ignatz Michael Neumann was a much admired and sought after architect in the 18th century, who applied his abilities almost exclusively to existing building structures. His solutions for the cathedrals in Speyer and Bamberg demonstrate a deep understanding of the historical and structural composition of the buildings. Out of this knowledge he was able to develop remarkable and specific architectural solutions that are regarded as some of the greatest achievements of the Baroque age.

Architectural design in the built environment, the creation of a qualitative and progressive design for an existing situation, has a long tradition. Good architecture is born out of and developed in the context of existing environments, drawing upon pre-existing approaches and developing them further. Many great designers in the history of architecture viewed architectural

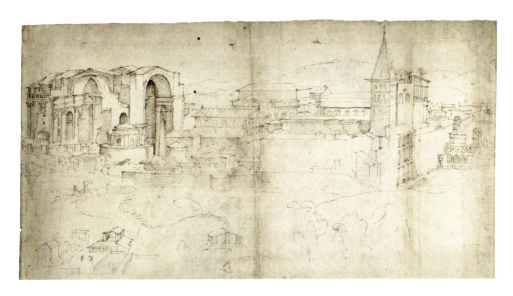

Even the greats adapted the works of other: the construction site of St. Peter's in Rome around 1535. On the right the almost completely demolished Constantine Basilica, left the new structure, at which several famous architects had tried their hands: Donato Bramante, Raffael, Antonio da Sangallo and Baldessare Peruzzi. None of the designs were completed. Without hesitation the great Michelangelo built upon their work from 1546 onwards. By the time of its completion, Carlo Maderno and Gianlorenzo Bernini had also contributed to the same building.

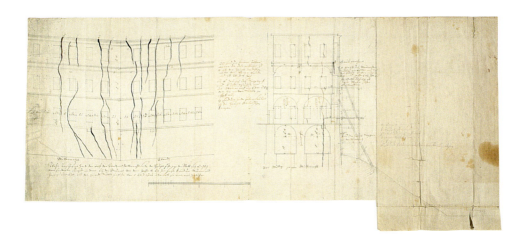

It has been well-known for hundreds of years that in order to design successfully in the context of existing buildings, it is essential to obtain a precise and comprehensive overview of the existing situation before beginning. This drawing from the 18th century charts the precise location of cracks.

design for existing built structures not as a restriction of their creativity but as a field in which to be at their most creative. Karl Friedrich Schinkel went to great lengths to emphasise the economy of his proposals for architectural conversions. For each of his conversion projects, he provided a plan of the original condition to allow the viewer to assess the changes themselves. Some of these projects are among his most outstanding and architecturally interesting creations. For the manor house for Alexander von Humboldt at Tegel, near Berlin, he respected the owner's wish to retain the old building, allowing its dignity to shine through whilst heightening its effect by cladding the existing tower and repeating it on the remaining corners of the building. His design for an additional storey that does not overwhelm the existing structure, and the accompanying unusual and brilliant solution for resolving the circulation and distribution of functions, is inspiring and a lesson for anyone faced with complex design tasks for existing buildings.

The built environment and identity

Our surroundings are fundamentally influenced by architecture. From the wider cultural landscape to the local neighbourhood, historic buildings determine the character and appearance of our environment. European and international cities are defined to a large extent by the form and arrangement of their buildings and these ensure that a place remains recognisable over a long period of time. The architecture governs the *genius loci*, the spirit and identity of a place. This term encompasses the persistent qualities as well as the current characteristics and potential of a built environment. The safeguarding and ongoing development of the *genius loci* is one of the primary tasks of town planning.

Buildings generally last longer than a human lifetime. Many survive several generations and some constructions, such as the Egyptian pyramids, even seem to have freed themselves of the shackles of time. The very permanence of buildings makes them predestined for use as bearers and points of orientation in individual and collective memory. Leaving aside prominent monuments for a moment, whole regions and cities are also defined by the variety and texture of buildings they contain, which although often of very differing architectonic or artistic worth, have become the bearers of many personal memories over the course of time, and therefore are part of the general collective memory as well. The importance of architectural continuity and the orientation it provides becomes particularly apparent where urban structures undergo rapid transformations. Where the pressure on land and property is high, such as in the centres of modern cities, the rapid flux of appearance and disappearance of buildings produces a nervous insecurity, which we compensate for with a stronger interest in historic processes. Indeed, in large dynamic cities such as Tokyo, London or Paris, the photo or film can prove a more reliable record of memory than buildings.

After periods of great loss of historic buildings, such as after wars and catastrophes, the need to reaffirm one's existence through architecture is particularly great. The rupture in continuity results in a deeper interest in the built heritage that remains. In Chicago, the great fire of 1871 was not only the occasion for the recreation of the city, but also for the definition of a specific local architectural language. In Warsaw after the ravages of the Second World War, it was decided to rebuild the city in a form that resembled the pre-war situation by rebuilding on the same historic building plots. The architecture that was built used a contempo-

Warsaw was almost completely destroyed during the Second World War. The rebuilding of the old city of Warsaw reconstructed what was lost without copying it in detail.

rary language but also alluded to the buildings' previous forms. The conservation of numerous war ruins after 1945 demonstrates the intensity of our confrontation with history, even and especially in the face of death and destruction. The authentic directness of the original fabric is much stronger than a story or an image.

The architecture of individual buildings is always a contribution to the general collective memory and accordingly is part of cultural remembrance. What informs the aims of the conservation of the cultural landscape or the urban *genius loci* also informs the architectural treatment of individual existing buildings. The conscious consideration of how architecture deals

In rural areas the faithfulness to tradition often continues unbroken. The old building forms are continued using modern materials. The ongoing maintenance and repair of personal property is a part of normal life.

with history is one of the architect's central responsibilities and one which he or she should not and cannot avoid. Of particular importance is to anchor a building in the current societal and historically conditioned discourse. Those elements of the existing built context that contribute to the identity of a place should be conserved, used and built upon. This understanding of the role of architecture is the basis for a culture that is both open-minded and rooted in the region. By drawing on tradition and developing it intelligently, the identity of the built environment can be strengthened considerably. Many European inner cities as well as the regional architecture areas such as of Vorarlberg or Graubünden or the work of such architects as Peter Zumthor or Herzog & de Meuron are proof of this. Architecture in the historic built context is a powerful expression of a European culture in which innovation and tradition are combined to produce a complex and varied living environment that is rich in character.

Old and new
The general public's relationship to the historical authenticity of architecture shifts continually. European culture in particular values not only the handing down of tradition but also of actual historical substance, be that buildings or artefacts, as shown by the active culture of museums and by conservation legislation. This desire to conserve is, however, ambivalent. On the one hand, the conservation of the historic built environment is pursued with an almost cult-like dedication and secures a meaningful environment. On the other hand, it is not possible to slow down the passing of time

and the aging process of objects and buildings cannot be prolonged indefinitely. The recovery of something that has been lost, the capture of a specific point in time or the reversal of the process of development is in principle impossible and also undesirable. The fact of death cannot be denied. In the mid 19th century John Ruskin wrote eloquently of the dignity of authentically aged building fabric. For him the aesthetic value of something was closely linked to its age, and this aesthetic value should not be impaired by modern intervention. His writings were a major contribution to architectural discourse and laid the foundation for modern conservation theory. Ruskin's ideas were taken up by the art historians Alois Riegl and Georg Dehio, who in 1905 argued that the conservation and not the reconstruction of a building should be the primary aim in the historical consideration of old buildings.

Modernism, by contrast, regarded adherence to building traditions from previous times to be a needless constraint on creativity and instead of tradition, posited fundamental renewal and asserted the right to innovate. Each generation should create its own environment and architecture should undergo radical renewal at regular intervals. Walter Gropius, at the time head of the Bauhaus, wrote:

"Given the speed with which technical developments have progressed in the last decades, we call for a change in the current practice to erect buildings to

The drawings by John Ruskin of palaces in Venice show the authentic aging of the building fabric complete with patina and traces of history.

Historical Roman finds fascinated the Bishop of Seggau, Germany, in the 18th century just as tourists today are fascinated by the ruins of Ephesos, Turkey.

last for hundreds of years. In this day and age buildings become obsolete much faster than in previous generations. For this and economic reasons we argue that the lifetime of a building should be limited. This would make it easier for us to finance new buildings and to remove obsolete buildings more quickly."

After the Second World War and the traumatic losses sustained as a result of the aerial warfare, the position of modern architecture with regard to history was again redefined. In 1964, the Venice Charter laid down a series of concise guidelines for the conservation of the built heritage that continue to guide our actions today. The fundamental message is that the evidence and information contained within historic architecture is valuable and irreplaceable and must therefore be maintained for current and future generations. To be able to hand down our knowledge of buildings, we must research and document them. Measures to conserve buildings should be chosen so that they preserve as much of the authentic integrity of the building as possible. In problematic cases the preservation of the building fabric should have priority over the preservation of its image. The Venice Charter also stated that any new measures, materials and auxiliary constructions should be differentiated clearly to distance them from the historic building or monument.

The interest in and appreciation of the legacy of historic buildings rose accordingly. The principles of modernist town planning had led to an emotional erosion of the built environment, to a rationalist indifference that could not be the aim of architecture. Social renewal, the preservation of historic town and city centres and the ecological movement entered into an alliance in which conservation was also an integral part. As part of the European Architectural Heritage year in 1975, criticism of town planning practices and the all too rational and uniform architecture it had produced became more pronounced. The built environment, and in particular historic town centres, were rediscovered by Postmodernism and rapidly rose to become a central aspect of design intentions. The historic environment, according to the postmodernists, already exhibits the complexity, randomness and character called for by new architectural movements opposed to the emptiness of serially produced, repetitive architecture. The built environment has its own innate *genius loci* which should be traced and strengthened. It also contains a variety of individual aspects, phenomenological fragments, whose relationship is no longer clear, and which can serve as inspiration, which can be emulated or contrasted. In practice, though, this approach often led to an arbitrary assemblage of historic forms.

Modern access and circulation structure for the ruins of Ehrenfels Castle, Germany (Auer/Cramer, 1995), additive and reversible in character.

Today the consideration of historical surroundings is standard practice and is ensured through a variety of design guidelines, participation procedures, conservation legislation and other regulations. Architectural and historical research has gathered together an abundance of material on the variety of types and forms of building and has furthered the understanding and classification of the construction and design of buildings. Nevertheless, our relationship to the history of our architectural past is currently being questioned once more. More recently, new tendencies have arisen that attempt to detach the relationship of memory from the authentic traces of the past. Taking up the ideas of the 1960s, they assert the right of the individual to freely choose a view of history independent of canonised interpretations. In the 1960s this may have been liberating; today it seems like a relapse into irresponsible arbitrariness.

What then does architectural design for the built environment mean under such conditions? What goals should the design of repair, refurbishment and upgrading measures have? How can qualities that existing buildings once possessed be recovered? Each kind of architectural design for the built environment is the communication of a particular attitude to the historic authenticity of architecture. It is well known that the portrayal of images, in the sense of a plain representation of an appearance, can easily lead to the unintentional loss of substance, and that the reconstruction of a previous condition devalues the historical reality as well as the present. On the other hand, society cannot and must not forsake the use of the memorial value associated with existing built structures. Many issues of how to deal with technical aspects of historic buildings, both in terms of construction and design, have to a large degree been clarified and architects can draw upon a wide variety of material in the search for appropriate solutions to specific problems. For Karl Friedrich Schinkel as well as for Le Corbusier, "learning from the past" did not simply mean emulating the past, but the creative development of and improvement on what has been achieved up to now.

The value of the built environment
Most people's opinion of old artefacts is contradictory. For many the old often represents stagnation and decay. On the other hand, the old is also viewed with a certain respect, recognising the fact that the aging process involves survival in the face of difficulties. The very fact that something has been conserved can stimulate wonder and reflection. Perhaps it is the familiarity of old things that one values, and the experiences which have contributed to their survival over time. The traces of aging can be perceived as a form of cultural identity. For John Ruskin, the attraction of the city of Venice was less the concentration of Renaissance and Baroque palaces to be found there than the visible evidence of the city's gradual dilapidation over hundreds of years.
The value of the existing built environment is therefore very much dependent upon one's attitude and receptivity to history and the historical legacy. The question of the attitude towards the old equates to the general measures of values at different times. Those who value only what is new will have a problem accepting inherited values. Those who think in economic terms and wish to make use and revitalise existing values will profit by making clever use of existing built substance. The role of respect and disrespect, and the awareness or ignorance of qualities and aspects of value becomes most apparent when short-term decisions have long-term consequences.
The built legacy should be seen not only as part of our cultural heritage but also as a material inheritance of society. From an economic point of view it is of immense value. Large amounts of energy are embodied in the building materials and in the construction, and these remain as part of the building until its destruction. Moreover, historic building materials from the

Architecture is an expression of its time. And time can sometimes pass rapidly. This office building in Berlin was renovated in 1999 and remodelled again in 2003.

time before industrialisation consist of natural, ecological and healthy materials and have proven their suitability over many decades.

Those qualities which differentiate historic architecture from modern buildings can often have an innate value which can no longer be recreated economically or without special means. Carefully hewn stone, intricate panelled doors or elaborate decorations are today no longer to be had off-the-peg. The expansive rooms, the grand entrances, the high ceilings and almost wasteful and creative use of space so characteristic of many historic buildings are very seldom realised for new buildings due to the high cost they entail or to building regulations. It is, however, precisely these aspects that many people value highly. Finally, the demolition and disposal of old buildings represents a further and often unnecessary action that also impacts on the environment.

Historic building materials sometimes require special skills for working them, but they are easy to care for and ecologically sound throughout their useful lifetime.

Old buildings have many inhabitants. Therefore, the protection of endangered species can also be part of the architect's task: bats in a restored gothic cloister.

25

The demolition of the foreign office of the former GDR in Berlin took place without any public discussion on the value of the architecture.

It is worth examining the different qualities that a historic building contains and their value in the present, and making these visible to the contemporary public. Done well, this can increase the actual material value of a property considerably. High returns can be expected by forward-looking clients who buy an old house in a less reputable quarter at a low price and, through their investment in revitalising the building fabric, transport its value outwards, improving the image of the quarter and strengthening the local building culture so that in turn the whole quarter improves step by step. By contrast, the persistent process of renewal without regard for what exists is uneconomical, as it discards the potential of the already available resources. As such, in addition to a cultural value, the existing built environment has a physical as well as an economic value that is all too often overlooked when decisions are driven by short-lived fashions. Clients with more foresight are aware that in order to maintain the real value of their assets, regular maintenance and sustainable renovation measures are necessary. Given that 70 – 80% of the built environment in 2030 already exists in built form today, society in general and architects in particular will need to consider the existing built environment, professionally and with a view to the future.

Further reading

Of the studies on the theoretical and philosophical aspects of time RICŒUR is the most concise. The discourse on memory was initiated by HALBWACHS in the 1980s. LÜBBE describes the problematic relationship of the present to durability. BREITLING/ORTH have presented collected volumes on memory and remembrance. Our relationship to the legacy of the built environment is discussed from different perspectives by ANDERSON, ASSMANN, ASSMANN/HARTH, BOLZ, BLOOMER/MOORE, BOYER, LOEWY/MOLTMANN, LOWENTHAL, LYNCH and TAUSCH. More concrete discussions of particular places and buildings are undertaken in CHOAY for France and FRANÇOIS/SCHULZE for Germany. MOSTAFAVI/ LEATHERBARROW provide a detailed examination of the decay of buildings. JENCKS re-examines the historic dimension for new architecture. ROSSI and LAMPUGNANI elaborate upon the meaning of the existing built environment for the city. OSWALT provides a concise overview of the motivations behind accelerated urban regeneration.

The beauty and intellectual value of old buildings is praised in RUSKIN'S 1849 *Seven Lamps of Architecture* and two years later in the *Stones of Venice*. BRACHERT attempts to objectify these emotional perceptions. The basic principles and approaches of conservation theory are best summarised by HUSE. Numerous aspects are contributed by WOLTERS. PEDRETTI, LIPP/PETZET and MEIER/WOHLLEBEN attempt a modern continuation of this theme.

CAPERNA/SPAGNESI provide a good overview of the historical extent of the task of architectural design in the existing fabric.

THE PLANNING PROCESS

Every intervention results in some destruction. Destroy then at least with understanding.

Luigi Snozzi

S˜pecial features of the Planning Process
The design process for working with existing buildings does not differ in principle from that for planning new buildings. Design principles such as functional usability, a high aesthetic quality and economic use of resources apply equally, if not more so. The most significant differences are in the more detailed initial research necessary, the greater number of participants involved in the planning process – most notably the conservation authorities in the case of listed buildings – and the more complex coordination of the individual planning stages that these differences entail.

Protective measures and essential repairs
Many projects in the context of existing buildings begin not with the project design but with small-scale building measures. A conscientious architect will want to ensure that the existing building does not suffer further dilapidation or vandalism during the often lengthy process of planning and negotiations. One of the first tasks for the architect is therefore to ensure the building is safe and secure, and that a range of precautionary protective measures are undertaken. As the market for reclaimed materials and architectural salvage grows, the risk that insufficiently secured buildings may suffer unscrupulous plundering or even wilful destruction within a short space of time has increased dramatically. Unauthorised access to the building site should therefore be prevented as soon as possible. A temporary site door and the bricking up of windows (maintaining ventilation) are better than the loss of original fixtures. Measures to protect against rainwater penetration are also essential.

Good and bad practice in securing buildings: ventilated below but sealed above and therefore susceptible to rot damage.

The broken lintel in Burg Witten, Germany, is supported by truss rods. An effective and reversible building measure (Hans-Busso von Busse, 1995).

Serious dry-rot infestation on the façade of the Narkomfin building in Moscow, Russia (Moisei Ginzburg, 1930).

Half-timbered wall construction exhibiting large-scale deterioration of timber members resulting from a damaged gutter; after completed repair work.

Blocked gutters and downpipes should be cleared immediately and any damage repaired.

Large and small-scale damage to the roof covering can be repaired with replacement roof tiles or, where this is not sufficient, secured with corrugated asphalt panelling or another suitably durable material. The effort required is usually minimal, and the protection it affords is considerable. Even a small hole in a roof can be the cause of major damage through dry rot during a half-year planning period. It is important to eliminate conditions conducive for dry rot immediately and not to wait until actual construction begins. Loose items already affected by rot should be removed and disposed of according to the regulations.

It is essential to ensure the structural stability of the building. Sagging ceilings and sloping walls must be supported in such a way that the load is transferred to structurally stable parts of the building. Monitoring systems should be applied to open cracks immediately so that building movement can

Electronic monitoring of building cracks.

be observed for as long as possible during the planning phase, and possible structural problems can be detected early on.

Preparatory investigations
Initial planning investigations for new buildings concentrate primarily on clarifying the urban context, the load-bearing capacity of the subsoil and, not least, the client's requirements. In most cases, a vacant site presents no further difficulties. Existing buildings are more complex. Over and above the specific measures described subsequently, a different way of thinking is also necessary. For example, making even small alterations to the building plan in order to achieve prescribed room sizes is not only costly but is in essence a fundamental planning error. The opposite approach is appropriate: What possibilities does the existing floor plan offer? How can the existing structure be used optimally, and how can the features and values of the building be best respected and brought to the fore?

It can often be more economical to abandon an envisaged usage in favour of a more feasible alternative, than to adapt an existing historic building structure to a pre-conceived use at great financial cost and involving damaging alterations to the existing building structure.

The level of planning detail
When planning a new building, an architect typically works from the whole to the part, and although desirable, it is not entirely necessary to have planned every last detail before construction work begins. When working on existing buildings, this approach can quickly come unstuck. In many cases, the execution of a particular planning idea will depend on specific characteristics of the existing construction, and these must therefore be determined in advance. It is not sufficient to develop a general idea at a scale of 1:100 for submission for planning permission, and then to work this up in detail at a later date.
The feasibility of a concept must be verified in detail at critical points, for example where a new staircase is planned, where walls are to be removed and for the routing of building services. This should be undertaken at the concept stage and special attention should be given to the building's structural system and to spatial interdependencies. Strengthening measures that end up weakening the existing building structure make little sense.

For this and other reasons, it is advisable to visualise and verify planned interventions in three-dimensional representations, particularly when these span several storeys. This step should not be underestimated and the additional effort is preferable to unforeseen or potentially disastrous consequences during the construction process.

Isometric drawing of new circulation for the historic building of Palazzo Lanfranchi in Pisa, Italy (Massimo Carmassi, 1980).

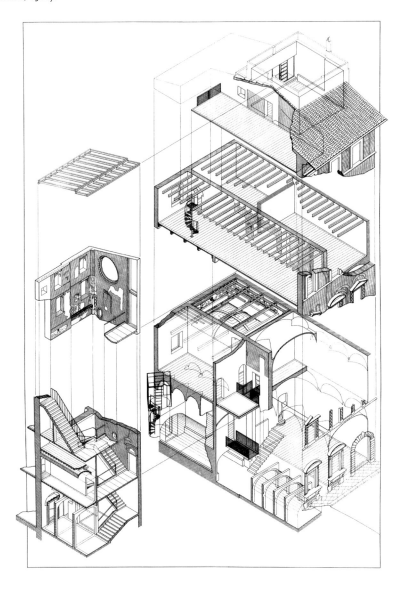

Sensitive response to the existing building

Conversion of the late medieval Casa de las Conchas to a public library, 1990s
Salamanca, Spain
Client: City of Salamanca
Architects: Victor Lopez Cotelo, Carlos Puente Fernandez, Javier Garcia Delgado

The 15th century palace played an important role in the rise of the Renaissance in Salamanca. All building works necessary for its conversion to a public library were based upon a survey of the building and a detailed damage appraisal. Through simple repair measures, carefully fitted to match the building, and only few new additions, the atmosphere and splendour of the original building substance pervades, whilst the room usage is left as flexible as possible. The design of new partitions, enclosures, ceilings, doors, windows and other fittings picks up aspects of the existing architecture and realises them using modern methods without attempting to contrast with the old. The use of traditional materials guarantees the best possible integration of the new additions to the historic natural stone walls and wooden ceilings.

The construction and design of the new windows fulfil the new requirements of a library but are integrated carefully into the existing façade.

Detail drawing of the façade.

The "rustic" treatment of the surfaces of new elements creates a similar material quality and simplicity to the historic building fabric.

A new window in an old seating niche with wooden grille, bottom-hinged window for ventilation and small wooden flaps reminiscent of historic shutters.

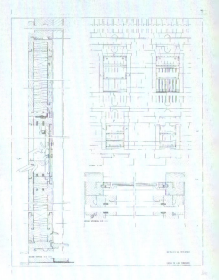

The Participants

The client

The client is always the central figure, the person who determines what should happen. Where clients have decided to invest in an existing building, one can reasonably expect that they have done so not purely for tax reasons, but consciously and optimistically and in the knowledge of what this entails. A favourable location, the historic atmosphere and any artistic craftsmanship of fixtures are often reason enough for such investment.

Interesting finds need not mean financial disaster for the client. Finds can be conserved behind appropriate protective covering. More extensive restoration is possible but not obligatory.

Nevertheless, the worry that unforeseen difficulties could arise is widespread among clients. The best way to alleviate such concerns is through clear and deliberate action. As ever, careful and thorough preparation is the most reliable basis for a project, and this will need to be financed appropriately. In addition, it is essential that clients are prepared to modify the envisaged concept to fit the existing building and that they have the courage to depart from standard solutions in order to achieve a convincing result. This does not mean sacrificing quality but rather an acceptance of the particularities of a building, its history and the resolve to bring out its qualities. This approach contributes to the individual uniqueness and unmistakable identity of a design concept, and is the reason why old buildings continue to be valued so highly.

Old buildings invariably contain interesting finds: plastered details, wall murals, concealed features and so on. The client and architect are not obliged to invest large sums of money in restoring such finds. On the contrary: when well protected, valuable finds can survive for longer. Conservation officers will only stipulate that suitable protection measures are undertaken.

The architect

The architect is the designer and coordinates all the other participants. Many more specialists are involved in the planning process for existing buildings than for new buildings. In many cases, expert appraisals are required to establish the qualities and particular characteristics of the building. These concern not only the structural soundness but also the properties of materials and the historic and aesthetic qualities of an old building. A high degree of skill and responsibility is needed to determine which expert investigations are absolutely essential and to avoid undertaking cost-intensive and even unnecessary expert reports. This includes avoiding duplication and ascertaining whether certain reports have already been undertaken previously, and if so, their validity. Architects must on the one hand avoid their responsibilities becoming fragmented into individual areas which are then undertaken largely independently of one another, and on the other hand resist the temptation to undertake all the tasks themselves, even if they feel able to.

The evaluation of the individual specialist appraisals and their interrelations and relevance for the later planning approach is the primary responsibility of the architect. This cannot and should not be delegated to others, whether the structural surveyor, who assesses the structural stability, or the restorer, who will wish to highlight the historic values and qualities.

The planning authorities

The requirements a new building is expected to fulfil remain strict despite continuing attempts at deregulation, and rightly so. It is quite clear that an existing building erected many years ago is not able to fulfil today's modern requirements. The architect will nevertheless attempt to reduce the number of deviations from current standards during the course of planning, however, in most cases this will not be entirely possible without either damaging the original building or incurring high costs for the client. For such cases, the building regulations allow the possibility of EXEMPTIONS AND RELAXATIONS in order that sensible building measures can be undertaken economically and buildings continue to be used.

Such exemptions generally apply to aspects that cannot be changed: low CEILING HEIGHTS, ROOM SIZES and FLOOR PLAN ARRANGEMENT, as well as the technical requirements of materials. For example, a historic timber construction must stay a timber construction, despite stipulations such as fire-safety regulations requiring other constructions.

In these times of increasing scarcity of resources, ENERGY EFFICIENCY is a further aspect. Many historic buildings have thick stone walls and these have excellent thermal properties. However, other parts of the construction may offer poor thermal insulation. Often, a holistic consideration of the overall energy efficiency of a building can balance out weaker areas. Historic windows can be equipped with additional secondary casements to fulfil minimal energy efficiency requirements and may then be accepted by the planning authorities.

FIRE SAFETY is another problem area. The requirement that all load-bearing elements of a structure should be made of non-combustible materials is sensible in principle. In practice, many old buildings, particularly timber-frame constructions with timber beam floors, cannot be adapted to fulfil such demands. Here the use of fire-retardant cladding and fire alarm systems can ensure that building inhabitants are able to evacuate the building in good time. In the comparatively unlikely event of a fire, the building itself or any material assets may have to be sacrificed. NOISE INSULATION is also an area where compromises are necessary.

However, in all cases, the willingness to compromise on the part of the planning authorities stops as soon as a threat to the life and health of the inhabitants can no longer be ruled out.

The historic window is fitted with an additional casement to improve thermal performance; the existing window remains in place.

LISTED BUILDINGS represent a special case. The conservation department of the local planning authority will be able to provide a list of which buildings are affected. All alterations carried out on such buildings require a special listed building consent. This may apply even if the measures would not normally require planning consent. Listed building consent is typically applied for in conjunction with planning permission, and stipulations in any consent given carry the same weight as other areas of planning consent. In addition to general building requirements, LISTED BUILDING CONSENT regulates everything which concerns the cultural and historical aspects of the listed building.

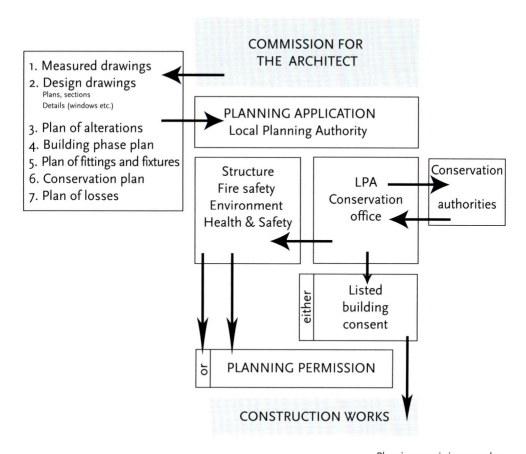

Planning permission procedure

In accordance with internationally recognised guidelines for the conservation of buildings, the conservation authority will in principle interpret every alteration to a listed building as a loss of historical information that affects its character and authenticity, and therefore also its conservation value. In practice, it is generally understood and accepted that in the interest of the long-term maintenance and use of a listed building, some degree of adaptation to modern standards is unavoidable, and even desirable. It is the architect's task to plan the necessary alterations, drawing upon his or her sound knowledge of the building, so that they are of LOW IMPACT TO THE BUILDING FABRIC and MAINTAIN THE AUTHENTICITY of the building. Such requirements are almost always fulfilled if a building measure is in principle REVERSIBLE. The identity of the building and its historic value must be preserved and passed on to future generations – that is all that is required. For

37

The building phase plan and plan of finds showing the historic complexity of the building according to objective criteria.

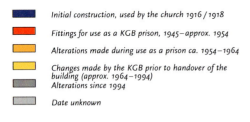

▬	Initial construction, used by the church 1916/1918
▬	Fittings for use as a KGB prison, 1945–approx. 1954
▬	Alterations made during use as a prison ca. 1954–1964
▬	Changes made by the KGB prior to handover of the building (approx. 1964–1994)
▬	Alterations since 1994
▬	Date unknown

(T1)	Door type (see room log)
(⌇)	Electric closure contact
(◉)	Spyhole: funnel-shaped observation openings
(⊞)	(Remains of) window bars
(E)	Electrical installations
(S)	Sanitary installations
(H)	Radiator
(P)	Plaster details: distinctive surface features, e.g. closure of openings or particular plastering techniques
Ofen	Fittings
(H)	
[Parkett]	Notes in parentheses denote past fittings and fixtures still evident in existing fittings.

Dashes denote either the existence of concealed constructions or where items have been removed.

38

The conservation plan details to what degree alterations are allowed based upon an assessment of the value of the building's features.

■	Very high density of finds, condition largely unaltered. Representative of earlier use as a prison. Overall context should be retained and not damaged by new insertions or fittings.
■	High density of finds, condition only slightly altered. Representative of earlier use as a prison. Overall context should be retained and not damaged by new insertions or fittings.
■	Low density of finds, later alterations. Less representative of earlier use as a prison. Overall context should be retained.
■	Original building substance and changes made by the KGB. To be retained as far as possible.

(T₁)	Door type (see room log)
(C)	Electric closure contact
(◉)	Spyhole: funnel-shaped observation openings
(⊞)	(Remains of) window bars
(E)	Electrical installations
(S)	Sanitary installations
(H)	Radiator
(P)	Plaster details: distinctive surface features, e.g. closure of openings or particular plastering techniques
Ofen	Fittings
[H] [Parkett]	Notes in parentheses denote past fittings and fixtures still evident in existing fittings.
	Dashes denote either the existence of concealed constructions or where items have been removed.

39

this reason, the conservation officer will want to focus on the principles behind the design concept – as will the architect. The aim of the conservation authorities cannot and should not be to overly involve themselves in design decisions, to demand the extensive uncovering of items of historic or artistic value or require the reconstruction of a previous built condition. The client may wish to undertake some of these of his or her own accord, and nowadays will likely meet with positive approval by the conservation authority if he or she does so. However, the authorities lack the necessary statutory mechanisms to enforce such requirements. That said, all those who too freely adapt an old building to their own purposes, retaining only an arbitrary historic flair, will quickly encounter massive problems with the relevant authorities.

The aim of conservation is the preservation, maintenance and long-term sustainable development of an old building. Opinions are divided on the merits of reconstruction: it has nothing in common with the aims of conservation.

Conservation is not the same as reconstruction. The "reconstructed Neumarkt" with the rebuilt Frauenkirche in Dresden was completed in 2006; it is not an example of building conservation.

In order to avoid problems and interruptions later in the construction process it is strongly advisable to provide more detail than the rather general descriptions usually contained in building applications, and to clarify in detail all aspects of construction that could be relevant to the aims of conservation. They should be declared in a conservation plan and described in the conservation concept. The often inevitable loss of historical building substance, however inconsequential it may seem, should be declared in a plan of losses that clearly shows the implications of the planning proposal for the building and whether the declarations of the conservation plan have been observed. Deviations are then easily identifiable and are an explicit part of the planning application. This open approach avoids unwelcome, aggravating and time-consuming discussions about the acceptability of individual building measures arising on site, even if planning consent has been granted.

From building survey to design concept

Naumburg City Museum, 1991–1999
Naumburg, Germany
Client: Naumburg Town Council
Architect: Johannes Cramer

The complex encompasses four burgher's houses from the Middle Ages and early modern era. Neglect had left the building fabric much dilapidated and badly damaged.
The historically important listed buildings were to be kept as far as possible in their original condition and converted for use as the town's museum.
An accurate measured survey and detailed element-for-element building analysis provided the necessary basis for conserving all relevant historic finds. Deficiencies were compensated for by additive measures, ranging from a new circulation tract to the structural reinforcement of the building structure and the levelling of the old and worn stairs treads.

The external wall of the old building adjacent to the new circulation tract. The old brickwork can be seen alongside the rendered lift enclosure. The carved wooden posts are exhibits.

Entrance area with additional binding beam for reinforcement and the conserved colouring of the ceiling joists from 1629.

Floor plan of ground floor showing building phases and detailing the plaster treatment strategy. Detailed information about planning intentions at the planning application stage avoids problems arising later in the construction phase.

The worn steps are levelled; the weak beams are given additional support.

Intricate repair work to a window frame undertaken by a craftsman. The carpenter's mark indicates the date of repairs.

The contractors

The success or failure of building measures will be largely determined by the qualifications and proficiency of the contractors. The intricate nature of planned works and the need to work with and respect the existing building structure and fabric mean that the majority of building measures will be the work of qualified craftsmen. Contractors must be prepared to undertake work with care and this should be both demanded and fostered by the architect.

Decision-making and communication

The complexity involved in working on existing buildings places greater demands on all participants than work on new buildings does. It is therefore all the more important that the architect maintains an overview of all aspects and reliably communicates all relevant information to the parties involved. Large planning meetings involving all participants, although increasingly common in recent years, are not always the most appropriate method; due to the many individual areas of responsibility, they can quickly become tiresome for those participants whose expertise may only be required for individual aspects and may not be requested at all on certain days. Instead, it can be more effective to coordinate individual measures in smaller groups and only to discuss the overall results in larger meetings. In this respect it is advantageous to provide a graphical summary in the form of plans and a centrally stored electronic room log that can be accessed by all participants.

Many building works may need to be undertaken while the building is occupied. In such cases it is essential to provide detailed information and to inform building occupants of works that may affect them. The purpose, process and results of works should be described as well as any disruption that may ensue such as noise, dirt and restricted usability. Again, the provision of more detailed information before works begin is better than discontent and disputes during construction.

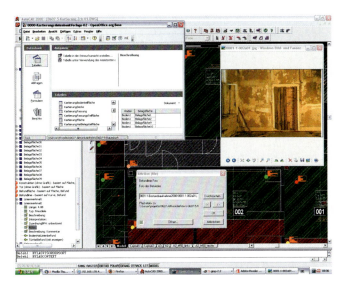

An electronic room log is a central depository of all information recorded about the building. It allows all participants to access as well as to update information; without doubt this is how building information will be recorded in the future.

Further reading

SCHRADER is a helpful reference for traditional building materials. Most literature on this topic is from the field of conservation. The issue of conservation-oriented planning methods has been a central topic in the field for many years, as has the task of repairing inhabited and otherwise used buildings. The works by ASHURST, BAER, FEILDEN, FISCHER, PETZET/MADER, THOMAS as well as WHELCHEL all deal with these issues. Also consult the literature discussed in the following chapter. FRANZ 2003 is helpful in questions of planning.

Stone-for-stone measured drawing of a gable with details of all finds, ranging from indications of alterations to remains of old plaster.

PREPARATORY INVESTIGATIONS

Only those who know the past have a future.* Wilhelm von Humboldt

Carefully executed and detailed preparatory investigations are fundamentally important for developing designs for existing buildings. Without thorough knowledge of the building, its specific characteristics and often complex structural interrelationships, it will not be possible to plan competently and therefore to avoid the unwanted complications that often occur later on in the building process: construction delays, uncertain planning objectives, spiralling costs and, in severe cases, even damage to the building or personal injury.

Although such problems are often conveniently blamed on the age and defects of old buildings, it is the job of the architect to foresee and avoid these difficulties.

The record of a building describes the physical fabric of an existing building in its dimensions and structural constitution in the state it is in as found. A building survey ascertains the changes in use and physical alterations the building has undergone during its lifetime, and examines its overall decorative and artistic qualities as well as its technical and material properties. Where the building is listed, its historic importance will also be established as part of a conservation assessment. Finally, an evaluation of strengths and weaknesses summarises the results according to a series of different criteria.

Without adequate analysis, it will not be possible to provide reliable answers to the client's three primary questions.

- Is the building in danger of collapsing?
- Are renovation and conversion works financially viable?
- What values should inform the work (economic, historic and idealistic)?

Collapse caused by a planning error. The famous collapse of the Campanile in Venice on the 14th June 1902 was caused by improper alterations made to the brickwork. The photo is, however, forged.

*Nur wer die Vergangenheit kennt, hat eine Zukunft.

45

The recording of the building and the building survey should be as factual and objective as possible. Interpretation and evaluation follows in a third, distinct step. This is where the strengths and potential of the building are identified and differences of opinion can be discussed. For instance, not every apparent defect may actually present a problem; not every defect needs remedying. An overview of all the findings provides the basis for determining the scope and boundary conditions for the design process.

Many aspects of the survey can only realistically be undertaken by specialists. Even where budget constraints are tight, architects should resist the temptation to undertake necessary investigations themselves or to delegate these to insufficiently qualified persons. The architect should also avoid excessively restricting the scope of the investigations. Savings made at this stage can be a false economy and may very often result in higher costs being incurred later on in the construction process.

The progressive degree of detail required with each step of the design process often results in recordings being taken in several stages. Checklists can be used to help structure the process. This approach should not result in approximate (i.e. possibly incorrect) measurements being taken first and then refined (i.e. revised) at a later stage. Instead, in the first stage the most important data should be recorded; subsequent stages then supplement and expand upon this information in greater detail. It should never be necessary to correct previous records!

As a result, the INITIAL INSPECTION can be undertaken using existing building plans or schematic sketches of the building. This encompasses a general appraisal of the structural system and any significant defects as well as a quick identification of valuable fixtures and finishes, and an overview of their restoration potential and, where possible, an exact dating of the building. The MAIN INSPECTION builds on selected aspects of the initial inspection, extending it with detailed specialist investigations and recording all information in measured drawings true to deformations and a comprehensive room log.

RECORDING HISTORIC BUILDINGS

The information accumulated during the planning process should be documented and archived in such a way that it can be passed on to future generations. Future building works will then be able to draw on and use existing building documentation. Should a building be demolished, the documentation will be the only record we have of it. For the archival of building documents, planning authorities and conservation departments require plans to be presented clearly with all necessary annotations and references for easy identification.

To ensure the long-term availability of building records, plans, photos and other documents should be stored in an archivally permanent medium. For example, drawings made with pencil on acid-free stiff paper have proven more durable than tracing paper, which ages not well. For black-and-white photographs, baryta photo paper is a better storage medium than PE paper. Glass plates are the most durable photographic medium and last almost indefinitely according to current knowledge. By contrast, the long-term usability of digital data such as photos, text and plans is as yet uncertain.

Property and geographic details

The development of a systematic record of an old building begins with the collation of all relevant information about the property. One should also establish which planning authorities will need to be consulted. Initial ideas for usage scenarios, access and conversion possibilities should be discussed early on with the local authority building control and conservation departments and, where applicable, the redevelopment agency. The title register provides details of rights of way or other restrictions and conditions affecting the property, and is available from the land registry. Public records and official documents may provide details of the age of the building, of alterations made, conditions or relaxations that apply as well as building plans and appraisals that have previously been undertaken. The precise geographic location should also be recorded (map grid reference or GPS) together with a title plan showing the plot designation and boundaries. Parameters such as the building volume, gross area and usable floor space should be calculated, although until a measured survey has been undertaken these may initially have to be approximated.

Finally, a reconnaissance visit to the building and its surroundings should be undertaken to determine the location of the property in its built context.

Documentary evidence and archives

A clear idea of the building and its environs is essential for developing a competent design proposal. After a first visit to the site and clarifying objectives with the client, the next most useful step is to research and assess any available literature in the archives. For famous buildings, documentary material can be practically inexhaustible. In other cases, published works such as the *Handbuch der Deutschen Kunstdenkmäler* by Georg Dehio or Sir Nikolaus Pevsner's *Buildings of England* and local topographical studies can be particularly useful. They provide a concise overview of the typical characteristics of a variety of types of historically important buildings. Inventories and gazetteers are a further source of comprehensive, well-researched information and the architect will usually not need to expand on the information contained within. For local documents, public libraries and County Records Offices are good sources of information. Further documentary research is in most cases unnecessary, particularly if time is limited.

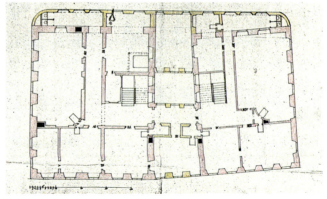

An 18th century plan for the conversion of the orphanage in Eichstätt, Germany. New structural elements were also marked in red at that time. Two buildings were combined to form a single complex.

The escape stairs are located behind the new façade.

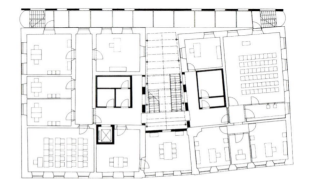

Conversion plans for the orphanage by Karljosef Schattner (1988). The Baroque façade to the rear was demolished and replaced in a modern form.

One can easily spend a lifetime researching in archives. It can be indispensable to track down and study archived building records. In countries like Germany and England the requirement to submit drawings with planning applications was introduced in the mid 19th century. Older building plans will only occasionally be available. Records of previous submissions for building works and alterations, granted or otherwise, can be examined at the local authority planning office, and in many cases they are sufficient to quickly piece together the more recent history of a building. For older buildings, further documents may be found in public archives such as the County Records Office. Permission may be required from the owner to view certain documents.

Plans from official documents can generally be regarded as reliable and any alterations marked provide indicators of where to look in the building itself. However, even a hundred years ago building projects were not always realised as approved and one should not blindly trust all plans. For this reason it is vitally important to verify them against the building itself.

Old records often contain interesting accounts: "14th Decbr. 1739 – a mason was sent up back and forth across the roof of the monastery's barns and storage buildings, replacing the odd tile here and there..." Maintenance is always better than repair.

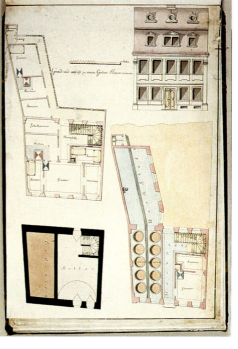

Building plan from around 1800. Hearths and fireplaces are marked precisely.

Although the information obtained from old plans may be correct, they are not generally metrically accurate. As a result, planning building works based on historic building plans can often lead to serious problems. In all but the simplest of projects, new drawings will need to be drawn up for a new design proposal.

An experienced researcher will be able to turn up further interesting facts from numerous other sources for many buildings, even those of lesser importance. Bureaucracy and record-taking was remarkably well-developed already 200 or even 400 years ago. However, for the layperson this direction of research may be less productive: it is not only difficult to evaluate archived materials; it may also be difficult to read the manuscripts themselves. Here specialist architectural historians can be of assistance. Early maps from archives such as tithe maps, and possibly also fire insurance plans, are by comparison easier to evaluate and can be obtained from the Ordnance Survey or local cartographic and records offices.

Recording the building as found

It is advisable to document the condition of the building before building works commence, for several reasons. Reliable documentation represents an invaluable reference when developing a design proposal; it is also an effective means of clearly recording the initial state of the building in the case of disputes. For such purposes, photographic records and a room log have proven particularly useful. A photographic survey documents the condition of the building, both in general and in detail. At a minimum, each room should be photographed diagonally from two opposite corners using a wide-angle lens to capture the entire room. Important details need to be recorded by taking additional photographs. These images should always be photographed containing a reference card for identification and a colour chart. The camera positions should be marked in an overview plan.

Each find is photographed with a record and colour card that identifies it clearly avoiding confusion at a later stage.

The ROOM LOG structures and describes the entire building. Traditionally recorded manually on survey report sheets, today it is increasingly recorded in digital form. The

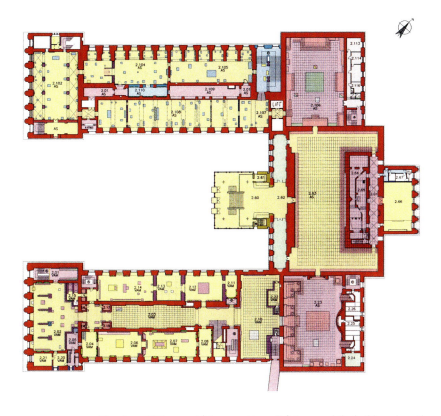

The plan of fittings and fixtures registers all fixtures and the building phase they originate from.

room log contains all relevant information about the building and allows the participants access to all aspects, whether for general orientation or for details of specific finds. The room log should be organised according to a consistent numbering scheme, which from then on serves to identify each part of the building. Every page of the room log should contain a standardised page head for easy identification together with a photograph of the respective surface and a supplementary drawing describing findings and their positions. The condition of each room is described in turn together with all immovable fixtures. Each surface – floor, walls, ceiling and exterior surfaces – is recorded individually. Extra sheets describe aspects such as doors, windows and construction details.

The ROOM LOG can be supplemented with further information as it becomes available, for example the results of detailed investigations or the invasive opening-up of building elements. The level of detail that needs to be recorded will depend on the kind of architectonic intervention. In recent

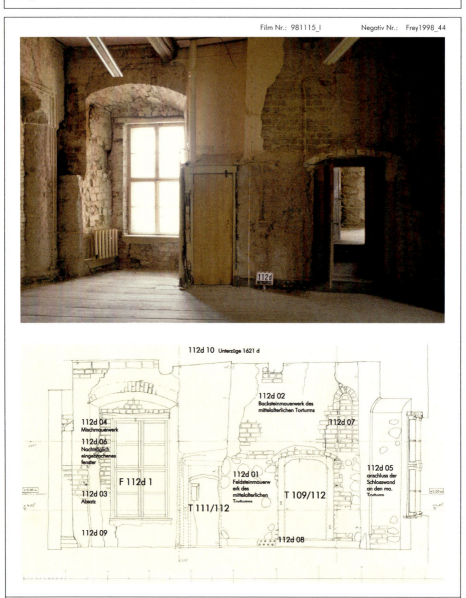

The room log provides an overview of the existing building. The consistent use of room numbers throughout the entire planning process is essential.

years, a number of checklist-based software packages have become available and without doubt they assist in the technical capture of information. However, they are not yet sufficient for the holistic consideration of a building with its qualities and weaknesses. The traditional analogue room log is just as extendable. The initial condition is recorded first, the subsequent planning is added later, followed by the final documentation of the end result. Internet-based room logs which can be contributed to by all participants in the planning process are currently in development.

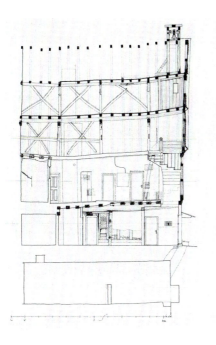

Measured drawing showing deformations (original scale 1:20) of a building showing severe distortion. The sloping floors have been levelled in the living areas but not in the roofspace. The cause of the problem has obviously occurred at ground level.

Measured drawing showing deformations (original scale 1:20) with building phases marked. The roof structure tilts markedly. Considerable packing was necessary to level the floors.

Finally, in addition to recording all the individual features in a room-by-room report, a plan of fittings and fixtures should be drawn up that provides an overview of all significant findings in summary form. As with the building phase plan, this plan should provide information about the age of the individual features using the same labelling system as used in the building phase plan.

Metric building survey

Without reliable building plans, every building project is destined to fail. The drawing up of the required plans is therefore the first step for every planning task. The precision needed in such plans depends on the condition of the building and the degree of interventions planned. Obviously, the plans for the repainting and minor refurbishment of a flat from the 1950s need not be as detailed as those required for remedying structural deficiencies in a medieval half-timbered house.

Incorrect or inaccurate building plans cannot be used as a basis for planning, and certainly not for building works. This would not only compromise the architect's obligation to provide accurate building documentation; such plans also form the basis for later facility management systems and rental agreements. In this respect, existing planning documents that predate 1945 do not represent a reliable basis for planning anything more than preliminary proposals.

The plan scale, degree of detail and the methods of a MEASURED SURVEY is determined by the precision of measurements required. In the field of conservation it has become common practice to grade building plans according to levels of precision which form the basis for specifications, contractual agreements and costings. The model presented here, as used in Germany, features four levels of precision; in Great Britain the RCHME has also defined four, slightly different, "Historic Building Recording Survey Levels". In this model, precision level I represents an approximate schematic survey; precision level IV describes the building complete with all deformations and the diagnoses of pathological investigations. The room numbers should be recorded in all building surveys regardless of the level of precision.

PRECISION LEVEL I: Survey at a scale of 1:100 providing basic documentation of the building type, its spatial organisation, elevation, form and external appearance. The plans can serve for preliminary planning proposals or renovation measures that do not require alterations to the building construction.

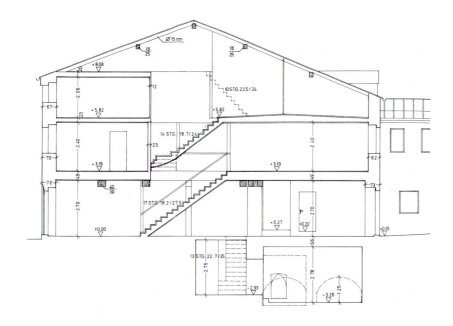

Standard survey of a medieval building in Regensburg, Germany.
Too simple: no evidence of building distortion – no damage?

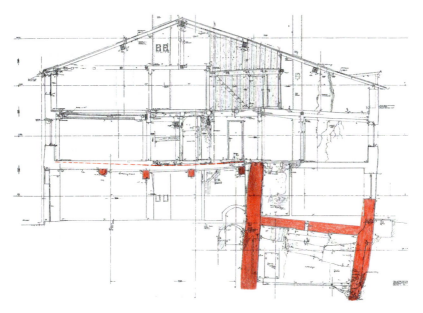

Measured drawing of the same building showing deformations.
Serious distortion is evident: building works will be complicated.

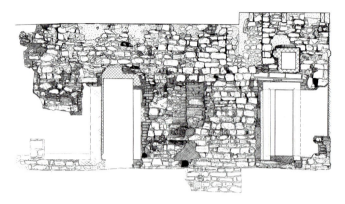

Analytical measured drawing of a section of the medieval city walls in Basel, Switzerland; hand measurement, original scale 1:20.

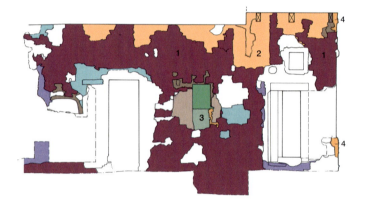

Interpretation of finds with building phases marked; digital drawing.

PRECISION LEVEL II: provides a near-accurate representation of the construction as-built at a scale of 1:50 or 1:100. The plans can serve as a basis for simple renovation works that do not encompass conversion measures, for townscape studies and as preliminary documentation for building and property inventories. Measurements should be accurate to within a tolerance of ±10 cm in relation to the entire building dimensions.

PRECISION LEVEL III: is an exact and geometrically accurate drawing at a scale of 1:25 or 1:20 and is suitable for building research requirements and for planning conversion works. In order to accurately record all building deformations, a three-dimensional surveying system is necessary, on which all measurements and detailed surveys, outdoors and indoors, should be based. Heights should be specified as metres above sea level. Floor plans, sections and elevations must be related to one another via survey datum points. The survey and plan drawing must take place on site. Measurements should be accurate to within a tolerance of ±2.5 cm. Where necessary, the actual measurements taken should be noted in the drawing.

As far as can be ascertained on site, plans should show the construction and structure of the walls, the direction of beams and joists, visible deformations such as sagging and slopes in floor levels, non-vertical wall inclinations, non-rectilinear room forms and, where visible, indications of previous building constructions and alterations. Where required, further details such as doors, windows or wainscoting covering the lower part of a wall can be indicated as simple contours.

PRECISION LEVEL IV: is a comprehensive analytical survey with all findings including details at a scale of 1:25, 1:20 or greater. It is primarily used for historically significant buildings requiring complex restoration and conversion measures, for building translocation measures (transferral to a new location), for structural preservation measures, for scientific building research and where building distortion is considerable. Measurements should be accurate to within a tolerance of ±1–2 cm. All surfaces such as floor materials and coverings, wall decorations and so on should be recorded as well as the results of pathological investigations of all kinds, particularly in section and elevation.

The selection of the level of precision required can have far-reaching consequences and the architect should on no account leave this choice to third parties. Unfortunately, this is all too often given insufficient consideration at the outset of the project, with the result that the same building may end up being surveyed several times over, first schematically, then more accurately and finally to a high level of detail in order to provide a reliable basis for planning. Quite apart from the delays incurred during the planning process, an attentive client will most certainly question whether the cost of repeat surveys is the result of insufficient or even deficient consultation on the part of the architect.

As a rule of thumb, the more complex and extensive the building measures will be, the more precise the plans will need to be. Buildings exhibiting significant distortions or requiring complex structural repairs make a true-to-form measured drawing necessary. The addition of new vertical elements, such as stairs and lifts, chimneys or service ducts will be difficult to plan without a measured survey that accurately describes the distortions of a building. Complex interior fittings often also necessitate precise measurements taking into account all surface irregularities. And even the partitioning of large rooms entails an accurate survey, possibly without the recording of distortions. What happens when the proposed minimum toilet facilities no longer fit as planned because the wall length is actually 10 cm shorter than shown in the plan?

In general when drawing up plans for existing buildings it is advisable to choose a scale that is twice as precise as one would normally use – for example, a scale 1:50 for the design planning. The extra effort incurred is not as excessive as it once was, thanks to computer-aided design.

Apart from planning considerations, good drawings make it considerably easier to reckon up with the various contractors once works have been completed.

The measured drawing represents the state of the building as found when the survey is undertaken. Additional interpretative annotations as regarding alterations and changes, for example, are interesting and desired. However, interpretation does not mean that supposedly less important information can be omitted in the interests of speeding up the process of surveying. This is important not only for methodical reasons but also in order to accurately record all planning data.

Whether the building is recorded by hand using pencil and measuring tape, or digitally using a laser theodolite or 3D-scanner, is in principle largely irrelevant. In today's computerised office environment, digital data recording will facilitate the use of the information later in the design process. By recording digital data in a system that can be updated continuously and by allocating all data to its precise position in the building, one can avoid the problem of duplicate measurements mentioned earlier. The traditional image of the architect setting off with a metre stick in hand to ascertain an overview of the building is now relegated to the past. However, the simple length by breadth measurement of rooms, even if using a laser distance meter, is not sufficient due to the high degree of approximation. Therefore,

Precision levels in measured surveys

Planning purpose   **Plan contents**

Precision Level I
Scale 1:100; Tolerance +/- 10 cm
Schematic survey of the entire building

- feasibility study
- deriving floor areas and volume
- facility management
- routine maintenance measures (only)

→ not suitable for design planning
→ not suitable for building measures

o only serious deformations
o only distinct irregularities in plan
o simplified representation of wall and ceiling thicknesses
o no fittings (doors, windows)
o no finishes

Precision Level II
Scale 1:50; Tolerance +/- 5 cm
Near-accurate measuring survey of the entire building

- functional planning
- planning application
- planning of works that apply to one storey only
- planning of works for buildings without serious defects or deformations
- planning of works for building measures not affecting the building's load-bearing structure

o deformations < 10 cm
o clear irregularities in plan
o near-accurate representation of wall and ceiling thicknesses
o presentation of the main construction elements
o schematic representation of fittings (doors, windows)
o main room fixtures (wall panelling, suspended ceilings etc.)

Precision Level III
Scale 1:25 / 1:20; Tolerance +/- 2 cm
Measuring survey true to deformations of the entire building

- planning of works for buildings with more serious defects and distortions
- planning of works for measures that span several storeys (e.g. lift, stairs, chimney, ducts etc.)
- planning of works for buildings with valuable building substance
- building measures in listed historic buildings

o deformations < 5 cm
o exact plans with all irregularities in wall paths
o presentation of the construction in detail
o building materials annotated
o detailed drawings of fittings (doors, windows)
o main surfaces and finishes (wall murals, floor finishes etc.)
o reflected ceiling plans (joist positions, plasterwork etc.)
o main historically relevant finds

Precision Level IV
Scale 1:25 / 1:20; Tolerance +/- 2 cm
Comprehensive analytical measured survey of the entire building

- building measures for historically significant buildings

o deformations < 2 cm
  All aspects of precision level III as well as:
o all surface finishes (walls, ceilings, floors)
o all fittings and fixtures
o all historically relevant finds

Precision Level V
Scale 1:10 / 1:5 / 1:1; Tolerance +/- 1 cm
Detail survey for conservation purposes

- complex structural planning in buildings exhibiting serious distortion
- detailed repair measures
- detailed interior planning
- detailed planning of restoration works

o all individual aspects of the construction
o all individual aspects of surfaces
o stone tooling
o wall murals

for almost all planning requirements regardless of the precision level required, the creation of measured drawings is generally undertaken by specialists, usually employing specialist equipment (although this does not preclude architects from acquiring such specialist knowledge). As a result, the architect will need to clearly define the services required of the surveyor. The definition of requirements for later design purposes can be as critical to the usability of the survey as the level of precision required.

Contrary to common practice, reliable measured drawings should not be drawn up in the office from more or less intelligible sketches and lists of measurements. Instead, it should be created and drawn on location. The measured drawing is neither a presentation drawing nor a working drawing. It has its own qualities, which are derived from the requirements of documentation and building surveying. It should be undertaken using a hard pencil (6H) on polyester-based drawing film, a 4H pencil on stiff paper (e.g. Hammer 4R) or with a tacheometer (total station) and laptop as a CAD-drawing. One should draw only what one has measured directly on to the medium without intermediate sketches. The pencil has proven a technically versatile, robust and durable instrument and is commonly used not least because it is possible to immediately rectify any errors. Film is dimensionally stable, i.e. does not stretch, and is resistant to tearing, to warmth and in particular to moisture (e.g. rain!). However, film is not entirely resistant to ageing. Documentation drawings (e.g. for conservation archives) are therefore often recorded on acid-free paper.

By drawing up on site, measuring errors can be detected and verified immediately. As the drawing slowly progresses from the overall reference system, the base line, measurement grid or traverse to basic data, internal structure and details, each step builds upon those previously taken. Errors become immediately apparent – the draughtsperson notices an anomaly and can track down the error by taking control measurements. Anyone who has attempted to locate an error in a drawing produced in the office or in hastily taken site sketches will recognise that, despite its apparent laboriousness, drawing on site may indeed be quicker and certainly more accurate. Drawings made on site also tend to reflect more of the character of an old building: the determining characteristics of the building are captured more easily and where the material qualities of surfaces are drawn, their graphical treatment appears more authentic. Drawing is in essence a personal study of an object. Observations, thoughts and questions which arise during the process of drawing can be recorded immediately as annotations. If the drawing made on site does not copy well, it can quickly be traced in the office as the original is known to be reliable. In many cases drawings are redone for particular purposes, for instance for the structural surveyor, for charting defects or as artwork for publication, and the layout and format may be adjusted accordingly.

The surveying of buildings is not so much a science as a craft. The methods themselves are relatively straightforward and by keeping the working process as simple and methodical as possible, the survey will be both more accurate and progress more rapidly. The complexities of buildings make the process more complicated, however with a little experience and routine the measuring process will progress quickly.

Given the widespread availability and comparatively low cost of reliable LASER THEODOLITES, a geodetic survey of a building will almost always be undertaken, not least because the surveyor's recorded data can be used directly for the later design phase. When undertaken correctly, the resulting measurements are not limited to a particular scale representation. The difficulty lies in the high degree of detail and in the accompanying poor visual clarity of geodetic survey drawings. However, a geodetic survey can contain a great degree of information on individual elements in one drawing and, in contrast to the hand drawing, these can also be organised in different layers.

DISTORTION-RECTIFIED PHOTOGRAPHS allow accurate measurements of planar surfaces to be derived, and their use has become more common since the advent of low-cost digital photography and a variety of user-friendly software packages. The dimensional accuracy of a rectified image applies only for a single two-dimensional planar surface, which should be flat and not be curved or otherwise distorted. Projections and indentations as well as openings and architectonic modulations will be out-of-scale as they appear overly distorted.

This limitation does not apply to STEREO PHOTOGRAMMETRY. This method can be used for the detailed recording of entire (scaffold-free) elevations and is particularly useful for detailed and strongly delineated façades. For the proper photogrammetric recording of buildings with more than three storeys, a crane-mounted aerial platform may be necessary in order to obtain unobstructed photographs of the upper storeys. Current photogrammetry systems capture data in digital form and, when carefully planned, the data can be used directly for the later design phase. Photogrammetry is rarely used for surveying building floor-plans, particularly since the advent of digital recording methods.

Today's high-performance computers enable content from different kinds of surveying systems to be integrated in a single data set. A photogrammetric or rectified image can be included in a sub-layer of the geodetic survey; likewise a detail hand measurement of intricate surface details.

The advent of 3D LASER SCANNING technology is changing the way in which buildings are recorded. Laser scanners employ a principle that is similar to that of the laser theodolite. Using a laser theodolite, each point is

Digital measured drawing with individual details of fittings and floor finishes arranged on different layers; on the left the layer structure on screen, on the right the plotted drawing.

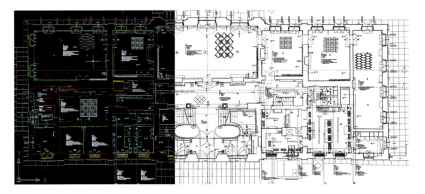

A hand measurement showing all surfaces. The drawing serves as a basis for reconstructing the 17th century pattern of use.

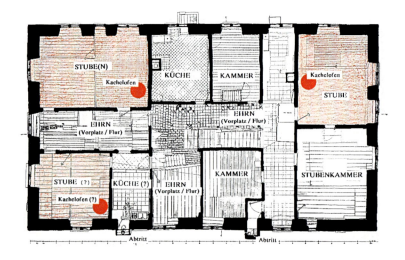

Digital measured drawing with building phases marked.

chosen and its coordinates are recorded one-by-one. The laser scanner records a large number of points automatically and in rapid succession generating a so-called point cloud with millions of points. A disadvantage is that to obtain data in a form usable for the later design planning requires considerable computer processing resources. Automated systems capable of producing useful results are not yet available; however, technical developments will most certainly make this possible in the near future. The advantage is that the point cloud contains a precise and complete image of the existing building fabric as a reference for the architect.

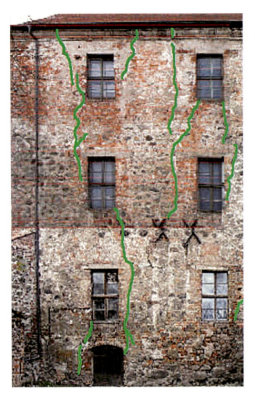

Cracks on the building elevation are marked on a rectified digital photograph.

For architectural surveying, the architect will need to decide upon the point density required to adequately record a surface. A point density of 5 mm is sufficient for accurate building surveys and detailed planning, and can be achieved by most currently available systems. The significantly more accurate STRUCTURED LIGHT SYSTEMS are not suitable for recording large surfaces due to their limited range, but they are useful for recording individual areas of detail.

The assumption that a particularly complex and modern approach will automatically provide more reliable results cannot be confirmed in practice. The skills, training and commitment of the surveyor will continue to be the primary determinant of reliable results. Therefore, architects should request references and samples prior to commissioning a surveyor. For comprehensive surveys it may also be wise to formally accept and test intermediate survey results (on the computer).

Stereometric evaluation representing all joints with two lines of a photogrammetric analysis of Speyer Cathedral, Germany, for use in the restoration of stonework (in this case additions and repairs).

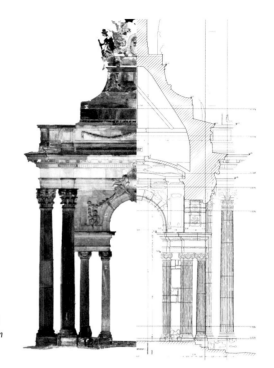

3D laser scan: on the left the point cloud as captured by the scanner, on the right the graphic interpretation of the data as section and elevation.

Building survey

The building survey reveals the relationships between the original construction and any alterations that may have been made to the building's plan, structure and fittings over the course of its lifetime, as well as any dangers or defects that may have arisen in the process. An understanding of the load-bearing structure is of particular importance, and the condition and technical properties of the building and materials are also relevant.

A systematic survey of the condition of a building and a diagnosis of all defects is a necessary prerequisite for the later planning process, not just from a technical point of view but also with regard to building costs. Without knowledge of the extent and implications of defects and damages, the architect will not be able to act professionally. What actually constitutes a defect is not, however, always as obvious as it may seem – besides other aspects, the assessment depends on the planning approach taken.

As with the measured survey, a systematic and methodical conditions survey requires expert knowledge and is usually undertaken by specialists. Whilst many may find it interesting to investigate and unravel the history

Not every defect is a problem: determining the history of the building structure

Houses on the Mühlenstrasse 2–3 and 4–5, 1999
Havelberg, Germany
Client: Havelberger Hoch- und Tiefbau
Survey: Yngve Jan Holland, Stefan Breitling

A thorough knowledge of the history of a building is vital in order to be able to reliably plan safe and sustainable building works. The original half-timbered building was constructed after the devastation of the Thirty Years' War in 1660 and is one of the oldest houses in Havelberg. At first, expensive foundation works were proposed due to the marked settlement of the building. A two-day building survey was sufficient to draw up the necessary documentation, to analyse the dates of the building phases and to clarify the condition and structural stability of the building. The investigation showed that the building was stable and had remained so for at least 150 years. The distortion of the building was the result of a fire and subsequent repair measures undertaken in the 18th century, in which the floor was levelled and the timber frame had been shifted. The expensive foundation works proved to be unnecessary; the investment in the survey and investigation led to considerable cost savings.

Street façade.

Rear elevation showing finds and building phases.

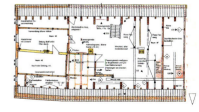

Roof plan.

Longitudinal section through the roof structure looking north.

Building phases

- pre 1660
- after 1660
- 18th century
- early 19th century
- after 1855
- 1st half 20th century
- After 1945
- Unknown
- Dendro inspection point
- Camera position

of the building, without appropriate knowledge it is all too easy to overlook important facts, damage valuable building fabric or recognise it too late as such. It is the architect's task to determine the extent of investigations required, which specialists need to be consulted (e.g. conservator, archaeologist, historian and dendrochronologist) and to define their activities appropriately and precisely. It is no longer realistic to assume that architects can cover all these fields themselves. Instead, an architect should have sufficient knowledge of the building survey to coordinate and direct all the tasks. Only he or she is able to define the requirements of the individual investigations and to resolve their interdependencies with a view to obtaining useful results reliably and economically. Clients will be sceptical about open-ended "research" that may result in lengthy, expensive and possibly even unnecessary investigations. It is therefore all the more important that the kind and scope of investigations are selected and clearly defined with a view to clarifying specific questions or problem areas. The purpose and form of specialist investigations and their relevance for the project objectives should always be evident, and although they will inevitably contain some jargon, they should be understandable and of use to other participants.

Building archaeology
A building survey begins by determining the evolution of a building, i.e. the phases in which a building has been constructed and the history of any alterations made. An understanding of a building 's evolution is a prerequisite for assessing the origins of building defects, whether manifest or hidden. The survey also reveals the cultural and historical value of the building, again, both where it is plainly visible and where it is concealed. For the architect, it provides information regarding the qualities of the building and its deficiencies. In order to stabilise the building, it is necessary to understand the building structure and any potential defects. Similarly, an awareness of the former spatial arrangement of rooms provides useful clues for the later design phase. For example, throughout the 19th and 20th centuries large rooms were often subdivided into smaller spaces – the history of alterations made to a building indicates where partitions can be easily removed to create a more useful or attractive building plan without requiring too much work and without impacting on the original structure of the building.
A historical investigation reconstructs the history of the building, representing the time of origin of individual building elements in plan, section and

elevation drawings that denote the original condition and the subsequent major building phases. The reconstruction should address the architectural history, any structural alterations made as well as changes in how the building was used. Naturally, such investigations will involve research in archives and reference literature. The building phases are commonly marked in drawings using dark colours for older periods and successively lighter colours for subsequent phases. Isometric drawings of the individual building phases help to communicate and understand the findings.

Even when it is possible to conclusively reconstruct the entire history of a building, this does not automatically mean that a particular previous building phase (whether as originally built or a later phase) has to be reinstated.

An archaeological investigation of a building involves both non-destructive means of analysis as well as techniques

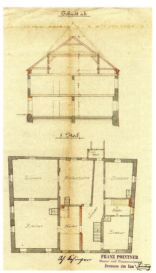

The plan from 1903 was used to obtain building permission and shows only some of the alterations that have taken place over the centuries. The remainder can only be determined by a detailed investigation. The building phase plan summarises the results.

pre 1504/05
approx. 1560
approx. 1600
18th century
1903

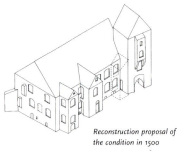

Reconstruction proposal of the condition in 1500

Measured drawing and interpretation of Freyenstein Castle, Germany. The accurate digital measured drawings serve as the basis for the building phase plan. By linking together the finds in three dimensions, the evolu-tion of the building can be traced, illustrated here in three building phase models.

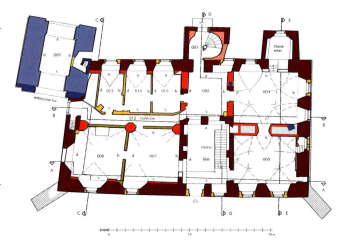

Reconstruction proposal of the condition in 1620

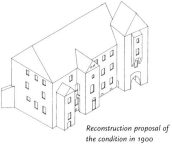

Reconstruction proposal of the condition in 1900

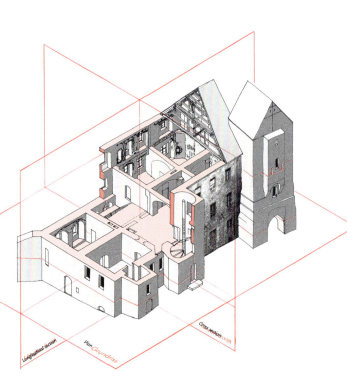

Documenting and understanding complex structures using a 3D digital survey model

Nidaros Cathedral, octagon, research project 1999–2004
Trondheim, Norway
Client: Nidaros Domkirkes Restaureringsarbeider
Project leader: Stefan Breitling

The octagonal apse at the east end of Nidaros Cathedral is one of the most interesting of its kind in a medieval cathedral. The early gothic building was begun in 1161 and later became an important destination for pilgrims in the 13th and 14th centuries.

The complex architectonic form made it necessary to represent the building spatially in three dimensions. The detailed measured survey, in particular of the junctions as well as of numerous details, provides indications of the design and planning of the choir. By analysing the settlement and distortion of the different parts of the octagon it was possible to date the different sections. A three dimensional tacheometric survey served as the basis for an HTML-based digital building information system in which all available documentation could be collated. The information could be made available to the different specialists involved in the monitoring and planning of restoration works.

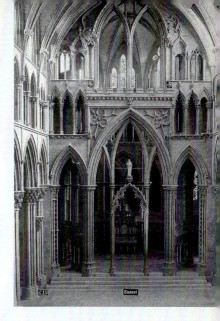

Interior view of the octagon looking east.

Section through the octagon of Nidaros Cathedral looking south; produced from 3D digital model.

Plan of Nidaros Cathedral.

Rotatable 3D digital model with database system and context menus providing information in HTML form. The picture shows the building ornaments. Rütenik 2004. System: Breitling 2005.

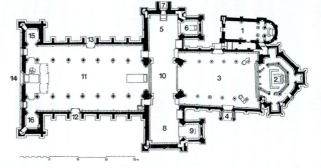

drawn from archaeological stratigraphy. Where destructive techniques are used, it is vital to minimise damage to the existing building fabric as much as possible, however seductive it may be to "delve deeper".

Historical building plans can provide first indications of previous alterations. An apparently irregular arrangement of different sized windows in a façade can point to a changeable building history. Distortions in the building structure may have been caused by a deficient building structure, and walls with differing thicknesses or changes in direction can indicate alterations or different construction periods. More subtle transitions can often be detected more easily with the help of sidelight. As a rule of thumb, similar patterns of change may often have occurred around the same time. Similarly, changes in building materials also point to different construction periods.

The location of concealed elements of the building structure can be detected using thermography. Although more commonly used to detect heat loss, thermography can also be used to reveal subsurface structures when the mechanical properties of the building materials are sufficiently different. Other remote-sensing technologies such as ultrasonic or microwave analysis, as seen in medicine, are rarely used, primarily due to the high cost involved.

Where the analysis of archive documentation and non-destructive methods show that alterations have taken place, it will often be necessary to open up the building structure to extend one's understanding of the situation. Such investigations will necessitate some form of destruction and should therefore be chosen with great care. Costs are incurred not only for the opening-up but also for the later reinstatement, and any damage affects the value of the building. In listed buildings such operations require specific consent. In all cases, openings should be kept as small as possible and should not impact on the overall appearance or the surrounding fabric. The perimeter of openings to be made should be clearly delineated and identified with a reference marker (see also room log). Widespread destruction of building fabric through the excessive or careless opening-up

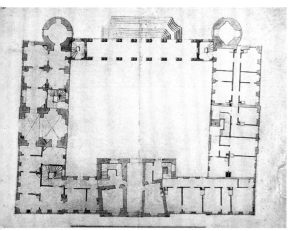

18th century building plan: the different wall thicknesses and their seemingly irregular arrangement indicate that the symmetric building complex incorporates parts of an earlier building.

of floors and walls, regardless of by whom or for what reasons, represents negligence on the part of the supervising architect.

The opening-up of building fabric, whether undertaken by the structural surveyor, timber infestation assessor or others, should generally be supervised by an architectural historian or conservator to avoid important building substance from being overlooked or inadvertently damaged.

The purpose of archaeological investigations is to clarify questions that cannot be answered by pure observation. Typically this involves opening-up seams between parts of buildings from different construction periods, transitions between materials or openings that have been bricked- up or otherwise sealed. Because such procedures inevitably result in damage to the building fabric and possibly also to as yet undiscovered valuable building substance, it is advisable to begin where damage is already evident, e.g. at cracks in plaster or where previous interventions have been undertaken. This strategy may also prove useful because cracks are often an indicator of concealed defects or finds. In this

Sidelight makes alterations and deformations more visible.

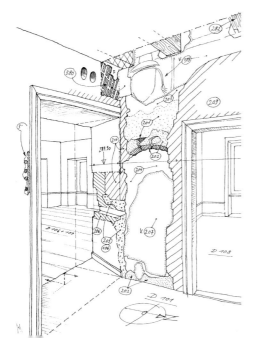

The spatial arrangement of finds is often of special significance. It is indispensable to show them in their physical relation to one another.

73

Gable after completion with a reconstruction of the colour scheme from 1627.

Interior view of the library with traces of walls dating back to 1627 visible in the floor.

New supporting structure with stainless steel columns and steel joists running the length of the building, profiled to reflect the bending moment.

Stone-for-stone measured survey of the gable with details of all finds, ranging from indications of alterations to remains of old plaster.

From defects analysis to planning concept

Heubach Castle, library and museum, 1991–1997
Heubach, Germany
Client: Heubach Town Council
Architect: Johannes Cramer

The aim of the project was to conserve the valuable 16th and 17th century interiors and to insert a modern use into the historic building. The former seat of nobility was erected in 1525 on the remains of an earlier building and in 1627 was subject to major modifications. Few further alterations took place and in 1983, when it was taken over by the municipality, much of the building substance was original, although suffering severe decay. The damage was so serious that the demolition of the building was considered.

The badly damaged timber construction has been strengthened through the addition of a secondary supporting structure of high-strength steel bearing beams and stainless steel columns. The structure extends into part of the second floor. An accurate measured survey was vital for both the planning and on-site insertion of the structure. The historic surfaces have been conserved both indoors and outdoors. The variety of different artistic finds that survived the ages could be conserved without the need for large-scale completion. Traces of the past history of the building have been preserved and have a subtle presence.

The existing building as generator for the design concept

Balbarini townhouse, 1989
Pisa, Italy
Client: private
Architect: Massimo Carmassi

The history and artistic qualities of this much altered townhouse were first fully revealed through a detailed building survey. The exposed walls exhibit clear traces of the building's past and the variety of colour schemes from different periods read like a lexicon of interior design through the ages.

The design concept treats the various historic finds as apparently random fragments of interior scenery and the lightness of the modern interventions is designed to contrast with the "maltreated" original fabric of the building. The new circulation requirements are achieved by introducing delicately detailed glass walls, thus adapting the existing building to its new use. The result is a stimulating tension between new and old.

The exposed masonry walls and the delicate stair together form a new layered space.

The fragmentary layers of wall decoration describe the long history of the house.

Detail drawing for the insertion of the glass wall.   *Isometric drawing showing historic fittings and new insertions.*

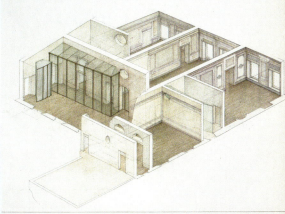

way several questions may be clarified at once. The relative age of walls in a room is best checked at corners where two surfaces meet rather than in the centre of each surface. Once a pattern has been established, it is not necessary to check every single instance, e.g. where vertical cracks mark the position of timber posts in the subsurface, one need not reveal each and every stud.

Building archaeology is a specialist skill and it would exceed the scope of this book to cover specific situations in detail. It suffices to say that aspects such as the composition of mortars, the effects of repointing, empty halves of timber joints in the roof structure and a plethora of other specific cases indicate to an experienced building archaeologist where alterations have been made, how the pattern of use has changed and when fittings have been added.

The thoughtless removal of plaster without prior investigation by a restorer has resulted in the destruction of a large area of old coloured plaster. Regrettably the result of incompetence.

A CONSERVATOR'S APPRAISAL is an external and internal assessment of the existence, condition and historical importance of fittings and fixtures associated with a building. Unlike the present day practice of fitting out interiors, in all ages and into the 20th century the wall was regarded as the bearer of architectonic and artistic decoration. Intricate wall murals, historic wall coverings, colouring and plasterwork are among the many different artistic expressions that are likely to be found in historic buildings. In many cases, such finds are buried beneath later layers of plaster or wallpaper and it is essential to systematically clarify the existence of original finishes prior to the design phase. Such investigations are typically undertaken by a qualified architectural conservator or restorer with specialist knowledge of plasters and colours. A conser-

Renovated interior with panel showing an older colour scheme.

Record sheet.

Successive layers of wall coverings can reveal interesting finds.

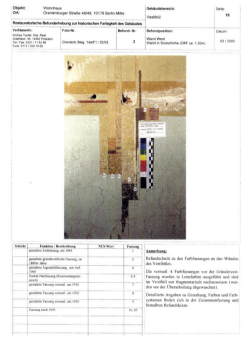

Exterior view after completion. Rough plaster is old, new is smooth.

From church to barn to cultural centre

Cultural centre in the Bernhard chapel, 1991–2002
Owen, Germany
Client: Owen Town Council
Architect: Hans Klumpp

Until 1999, an unprepossessing farmhouse stood on the edge of the market place in the town of Owen. In 1877 an obsolete tithe barn, which had originated from an earlier church that had survived after the Reformation, had been turned into the farmhouse. Two extensive frescoes with medieval wall murals had survived all later alterations, hidden behind stacks of hay and thick layers of plaster. It was damaged and incomplete but still legible in structure and in details. The design concept opened up the entire area of the former nave. All new additions are clearly recognisable as being 'modern'. In a complex restoration process, the historically important wall murals were carefully revealed, cleaned and in parts retouched to improve legibility. For experts it is easy to distinguish between the original and the retouched areas. The building now serves as a clubhouse and public space for cultural activities.

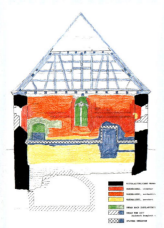

Analytical cross section based upon a stereo-photogrammetric survey showing the building phases and wall murals.

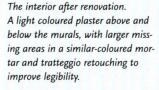

The interior after renovation. A light coloured plaster above and below the murals, with larger missing areas in a similar-coloured mortar and tratteggio retouching to improve legibility.

The condition of the murals after uncovering, cleansing and retouching.

Reconstruction of original colour scheme

Schminke house, 1933/2000
Löbau, Germany
Client: Wüstenrot Foundation
Architect: Hans Scharoun/Pitz & Hoh

The Schminke house by Hans Scharoun is regarded as a milestone of 20th century architecture due to its radical and uncompromising design. The not entirely adequate building techniques of the time and years of neglect had left the house in a sorry state. The renovation concept aimed to restore the authentic substance of the building whilst respecting later modifications. The intention was to draw on an almost complete knowledge of the building and the history of the alterations made. Of primary concern was the legibility of Scharoun's floor plan and the delicate colour scheme he had developed. With the help of a detailed conservator's analysis, it was possible to reconstruct the entire original colour scheme. The renovation concept demonstrates an awareness of the ongoing history of a building, and the original condition was not restored throughout. The historic colour scheme was restored only in sections of the building.

Interior after restoration and reconstruction of the original colour scheme.

View of the building after completion in 1933.

Detail of conservator's analysis of the historic colour scheme.

Cleansed area of external render showing the original colouring.

Entrance area with reconstruction of the historic colour scheme.

vator will also be able to interpret the successive layers of plaster and paint with regard to the chronology of the building. Again, care should be taken here not to damage large areas of existing building fabric with rough tools – a breach of basic rules of the discipline. As a specialist for materials, the conservator will also be able to analyse historic mortars and to manufacture similar mortars for repairs. Likewise, if historic colour schemes are to be restored, the conservator can advise on the appropriate composition of historic colours and traditional materials.

As old buildings rest on old soil, one should be aware that any earthworks undertaken may reveal FINDS OF ARCHAEOLOGICAL INTEREST. Even the renewal of connections to utilities may turn up finds, and these must generally be examined by the local authority archaeological department. If relevant finds are discovered, be they the remains of graves, artefacts or parts of previous buildings, the local authority should be notified. The assessment of the significance of finds should be left to the archaeologists. Finds may be discovered both outdoors and indoors, for example evidence of former production facilities. If a find proves interesting the immediate surroundings will be examined to determine the extent of other possible finds before a full archaeological excavation is undertaken. It can therefore be advisable to undertake an archaeological investigation prior to commencement of building works in order to avoid unwelcome delays later in the building process.

Archaeological find discovered under the floor at ground level. Some of the tanning pits from around 1700 still contain their original contents.

Most buildings will contain some smaller finds that may provide clues to the cultural and historical use of the building. Whether a lost trouser button, items concealed within walls or a cache of discarded crockery, these finds reveal a lot about the identity and the uses of an old building. For receptive owners or clients, this can add further meaning to their project.

The desire to conclusively determine the age of a building and any subsequent building phases using a variety of DATING METHODS is widespread, although strictly speaking it is of secondary importance for the planning process. For centuries, the dating of a building according to STYLISTIC PERIOD has served as a primary means of determining the approximate age. Experienced architectural historians will be able to draw well-reasoned conclusions, although a potential for substantial error always remains. DOCUMENT-BASED DATING can be misleading: written evidence may not necessarily refer to the building fabric as it exists in the present day and dates given in documents should not be blindly trusted. INSCRIPTIONS can be more reliable but here too a potential for error can still exist. It was not uncommon to re-use old building materials in a later building, including those with inscriptions, and it is also known that inscriptions were sometimes added at a later date.

DENDROCHRONOLOGY or tree-ring dating is a much more reliable indicator. When undertaken correctly, an analysis of the annual growth rings of construction timbers enable one to determine the age of the wood precisely. Where in the past entire cross-sections were removed for analysis, today

Over a long period of time, broken crockery has been thrown through the narrow window into an inaccessible space.

Piecing together the shards sheds light on the everyday life of the earlier inhabitants.

81

The reliability of evidence! How can one explain both dates above the door?

Dendrochronology. The distance between the annual rings differs according to the climate of each year. A long succession of tightly and widely spaced rings never occurs repeatedly. By analysing historic climate data one can determine when the tree grew from its core to bark.
The removal of a cross-section of a beam provides a good overview but destroys the beam in the process. A drill core (marked B1 and B2) preserves the overall integrity of the beam. The uneven growth of the annual rings means that the absolute distances between annual rings from two drill cores can differ. The pattern of wide and narrow bands is however the same.

small timber drill core samples are taken resulting in far less damage to the building substance. Both the taking of core samples and their subsequent analysis are the work of specialists and specialist laboratories.

Given the general interest in determining the exact date of a building, the investment in a dendrochronological analysis is almost always worthwhile. Other scientific dating methods such as thermoluminescence dating (for dating brickwork), radiocarbon dating, also known as carbon-14 dating (for organic materials) or optically stimulated luminescence (OSL, for mortars) are less commonly used due to the complicated sampling and lengthy analysis procedures as well as the high costs and relatively imprecise results.

Structural survey

A structural survey ascertains the general structural stability of an existing building, any deformations or distortions of the building structure and the interdependencies of individual building elements, which can be particularly complicated when a building has undergone a series of alterations. A comprehensive and precise survey of the load-bearing structure, describing its characteristics, potential capacity and all deficiencies is an essential part of building investigations and their representation in clear plans is a prerequisite for understanding the building structure. Serious damage can result when supporting walls are opened up, concealed structural members are cut through or supplementary strengthening measures are removed because one is unaware of their role or they are judged to be of secondary importance. A structural appraisal collates all information relevant for the later design phase such as the direction a ceiling spans or the location of immovable structural elements. A carefully executed historical investigation of the building as described earlier will also be able to determine whether defects that appear to be drastic are in fact the result of damage that the building sustained a long time ago, and therefore possibly are no longer serious.

An investigation of the load-bearing structure is therefore only complete once both the original structure and all subsequent alterations, together with any resulting structural implications, have been deter-

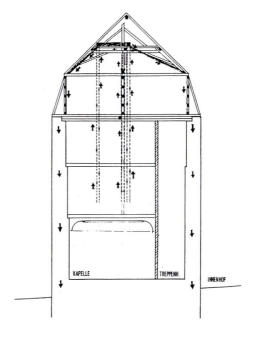

Without precise knowledge of the building even a small alteration can lead to disaster. The ceiling of the chapel on the ground floor of Idstein Castle, Germany, is suspended from iron bands that hang from the roof. Caution is called for before carelessly sawing through what might at first appear to be an obstacle.

mined. Historic load-bearing systems are generally straightforward constructions designed to withstand normal compression and tension. Complex technical engineering constructions are a more recent phenomenon and even today are less common. Accordingly, with the help of the building phase plan, it is generally not difficult to determine the original structural system in the majority of cases. It becomes more complex when later alterations have affected the building's structural mechanisms. In many half-timbered buildings, "bothersome" braces and struts have been removed as part of modernisation measures, impairing the building's ability to withstand distortion. Openings made in supporting walls may affect how load is distributed across the rest of the structure. Inappropriate repairs may not adequately fulfil the original purpose and material fatigue contributes to structural weakness. In many cases, previous deficiencies may have been solved through additional strengthening measures and likewise it is not uncommon to find that whole sections have been replaced in the past. All such developments also need to be determined as part of the survey. Only once one has gained a full appreciation of the structure of a building can one repair or alter the structure appropriately. This principle is commonly used when analysing the subsoil of a plot of an old or new building and should be also adopted when working on existing buildings.

As proof of a full understanding of the original structure and any subsequent alterations, the load-bearing system should be reconstructed as a drawing illustrating the different building phases and their structural systems.

For the ASSESSMENT OF STRUCTURAL STABILITY and load-bearing capacity of historic building structures as well as of margins of safety, the structural engineer can draw upon a whole series of calculation models. The structural performance of many historic constructions has been systematically assessed and engineers will usually be able to base their investigations on these standard values without needing to ascertain the actual performance of every structural member in the building, although all models can only be an approximation of the actual conditions on site. However, more important than the determination of individual material characteristics is an understanding of the overall constructive interdependencies and relationships of structural components. For example, structural movement is generally undesirable though in some cases it can be better to observe the pattern of movement over an extended period of time and to accept it rather than to intervene too hastily in a delicate construction that is gradually coming to rest.

Distortions that become evident in the measured survey and an analysis of cracks in plasterwork provide a first indication of possible defects in the STRUCTURAL SYSTEM. Not every crack or distortion is necessarily serious but they should be examined carefully. In particular, cracks that are evident in the uppermost layers of a building indicate probable ongoing movement. Where more recently applied finishes over previous cracks have remained intact, this indicates that the cause of damage has probably stabilised. Vertical cracks, especially in the corners of rooms, may be less dramatic than diagonal shearing cracks across wall surfaces that may result from uneven settlement or load redistribution. In order to properly assess their significance, cracks should be charted across several stories. The extent and seriousness of distortions often becomes evident as a result of systematic mapping, e.g. the recording of height notations or the use of vectors. Cracks follow the path of least resistance and it is common to see them traverse wall openings. Cracks that appear in conjunction with bulging walls are almost always a warning signal. The degree of deformation or distortion and therefore the implications for structural stability can be determined by levelling which should be undertaken as part of the measured survey. One should be aware that older buildings can exhibit complex patterns of

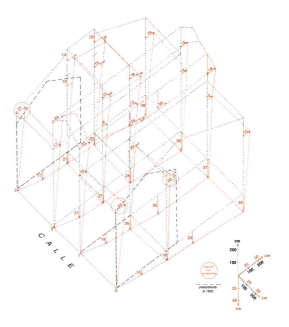

Analysis of distortions in a residence in Venice. By determining the degree of deviation from the horizontal or vertical, problem areas can be quickly visualised.

Serious problems: The gable wall has collapsed previously and been rebuilt. The tie rods barely hold together the building and new cracks have already started appearing.

85

distortion and it is advisable to monitor the movement of a building structure for a longer period of time. The seasons or other climatic changes can often have an effect on the building, and meaningful results can only be obtained by monitoring movement for at least one year.

Serious distortions of floors and ceilings are almost always a sign of ongoing structural problems. Insufficient bracing can lead to skews in buildings, sagging floors can result from the removal of supporting walls in the floor below and decaying timber pile foundations can cause settlement: the list of possible causes can be extensive. However, aside from those mentioned, in most cases the most serious structural damage results from inappropriate interventions made to the building structure.

Another cause of structural defects in an otherwise intact structural system is material fatigue or fungal or beetle infestation. The extent, cause and implications of rusty iron in steel constructions, corroded reinforcement rods in concrete and organic infestation of timber structures must be conclusively examined before the architect or surveyor is able to assess the structural stability or estimate the cost of necessary remedial works. It is therefore essential to examine the technical and mechanical properties of building materials. An investigation of building defects in historic buildings is at the same time an examination of the history and cause of defects. If damage is repaired but the cause is not remedied, further cost-intensive repairs will almost certainly follow. A replacement for a decayed floor joist will also gradually decay if the source of water ingress is not remedied, e.g. a cornice that directs water into instead of away from the masonry. Similarly, reapplied plaster will flake off repeatedly if the rusty iron lintel it conceals is not properly treated.

Technical and material investigations

An inspection of the technical and material properties of parts of the building construction aims to identify the kinds of materials used in the building and their respective conditions. As with the structural survey, a diagnosis of the cause of defects, together with an appraisal of the risk of future damage and the means of avoidance are central aspects. A materials inspection takes into account not only damage to the building structure and shell (e.g. rising damp) but also the condition of fittings and fixtures (e.g. plasterwork over hollowed out subsurfaces, the condition of windows and floors). Although the identification and recording of such details at this stage may seem laborious, it proves valuable later when it comes to quantifying the extent of necessary renovation measures.

As with all investigations, it can be more cost-effective to first undertake an initial inspection in order to identify the necessity and purpose of further investigations.

The extent and effects of material sampling should be considered and stipulated in advance of the inspection. Not all specialists will be sensitive to the value of the existing built fabric and without guidance unnecessary damage can occur as a result of material sampling.

Non-destructive diagnosis of the structure beneath the render using thermography.

"Over-enthusiastic" sampling damages the building. The degree shown here is excessive, even for complex situations.

The extent of investigations necessary to diagnose the specific problems encountered should be determined at the outset, i.e. whether investigations are to be non-destructive, semi-destructive or destructive. In many cases it will be sufficient to inspect and record damages visible on the surface. For construction elements that are concealed beneath surfaces, a number of non-destructive techniques exist, most notably thermography which allows materials with different surface temperatures to be detected beneath plaster. The same method is commonly used to detect heat loss or measure the effectiveness of insulation material.

Historic buildings up until the mid 20th century are built from materials whose properties we know well. Nevertheless, each type of building, each type of construction and each material has its own specific characteristics and susceptibilities to environmental conditions, moisture, weathering, material fatigue and other potentially damaging external influences. Particular attention should be given to the durability and potential for defects of comparatively recent constructions and materials, most notably reinforced concretes and plastics whose longevity has not yet been proven over hundreds of years.

In general a materials inspection will examine the structural stability of a material, its robustness, any possible material loss, moisture content, chemical damage and organic decay. As residual moisture is one of the most common causes of building defects, an analysis of water penetration and points of ingress is especially important. This includes external conditions such as ground water level, soil moisture levels, water seepage, rainfall, surface water and splashing as well as internal sources of moisture such as condensation and vapour diffusion.

FALLACY: "Saltpetre" erodes masonry
Rising damp from the ground that travels upwards through masonry also transports soluble salts. When the moisture evaporates the salt crystallises increasing in volume by a factor of seven. If this happens in render and plaster or near the surface of brickwork, it will cause the surface layer to flake and fall off, a process known as spalling. Cement render is commonly applied in an attempt to contain the problem; however, all this does is simply push the moisture further upwards.

In addition to structural stability, thermal transmission properties, wind-resistance and acoustic insulation are further relevant material properties. Only in exceptional circumstances will it actually be necessary to test the properties of a material, e.g. the quality of timber or compression strength of stone masonry. Instead, where the properties of constructions or materials are deemed inadequate, additional secondary measures may be undertaken to compensate. In most cases, investigations will aim at confirming the structure and composition of materials. This helps not only to assess the quality of the building construction as well as its expected durability, but also to select complementary and appropriate materials for repair measures. Detailed material investigations are undertaken by specialist laboratories, product manufacturers or certified materials surveyors. In addition to the accredited materials testing institutes, a number of independent laboratories offer analytical services often with a rapid turnaround. Drawing upon vocabulary more commonly used in medicine, they offer early detection and holistic appraisal services for processes damaging the existing building fabric. Given that the architect will not be able to reliably investigate such aspects him- or herself, attention should focus on the purpose of investigations and the formulation of questions that need clarification. This enables the architect both to determine the extent of necessary investigations as well as to assess the relevance and implications of the results.

The damage continues on upwards unavoidably behind the cement "repairs". It would have been better to leave as it was.

The analysis of building defects should be undertaken methodically and on larger surfaces. An isolated examination of the centre of an area of serious damage can skew the overall picture in which, despite an area of major damage, a large part of the building may remain unaffected. The measured drawings serve as the basis for a SURVEY OF DEFECTS. The survey of defects charts building damage categorised according to a consistent pattern so that the plan drawings provide a compact overview of the overall situation. It is advisable to restrict the number of categories as far as is practicable. In most cases, more than three category colours in addition to the defect-free area will not be necessary. Major damage is usually marked in dark red so that the plan already provides a clear graphic indication of those areas where most building measures will be necessary and changes are unavoidable. Mapping damaged areas also helps to objectively assess the overall extent of damage, which may in actual fact be less than originally thought: serious defects often dominate the impression of a building on site; few people see how much of the building is free of damage.

EVALUATION AND INTERPRETATION – STRENGTHS AND WEAKNESSES
The results of historical research, the building survey and the different investigations undertaken need to be compiled into an overall report which provides a clear overview of the information obtained and their implications for the planning objectives. The report should be comprehensible to all participants: a pile of individual specialist appraisals is of little help when the interrelationships between them and their relevance for the project are not

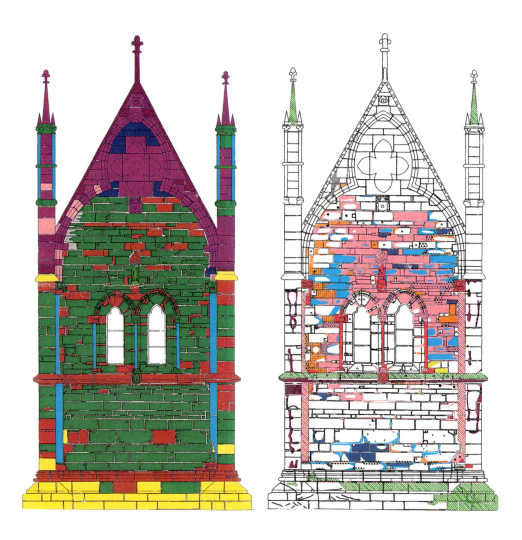

The systematic survey of Trondheim Cathedral, Norway, differentiates between the objective recording of data (left: types of stone) and its assessment (right: defects). The two drawings depict the same thing but convey different information. Certain kinds of stone weather more quickly than others. The plinth is subject to greater wear than the gable. A causal relationship is not automatic.

made clear. This should take the form of an evaluative summary that describes the qualities of the building and its deficiencies. It is one of the architect's central tasks when dealing with existing buildings.

Discussions concerning the re-use of historic buildings can often become contentious, and it has proven useful to describe both the facts and their evaluation not only verbally but also in the form of plan representations. These provide an objective summary of factual and verifiable information and, should discussion arise, enable an evaluation of the implications using objective criteria.

1. BUILDING PHASE PLAN

As described on p. 69. No other plan provides such an immediate overview of the original building and the alterations it has undergone over its lifetime. In addition, a spatial visualisation of alterations and the phase-by-phase evolution of the building volume are often particularly informative.

2. PLAN OF DAMAGES

As described on p. 89. Here too, a plan summarising all the individual building defects recorded provides the best possible overview of the condition of a building. Areas in which defects are most evident, whatever they may be, will be those areas requiring major building works. This will often be where new interventions, for example to adapt the building to a new use, can be undertaken without causing any conflicts. Conversely, planning measures should endeavour not to impact upon areas without any damage.

3. PLAN OF FITTINGS AND FIXTURES

A carefully planned design will attempt to conserve and bring out the qualities of a building. Accordingly, major interventions should not be undertaken where valuable fixtures and finishes are intact and complete. A plan of fittings and fixtures provides an overview of areas where valuable finds exist and interventions are best avoided and where they can be undertaken with less impact on the building.

In many cases the plan of fittings and fixtures has been reduced to a map of positives in which only those building elements of particular relevance for the further planning process are mapped, leaving out less significant observations. Whilst this approach concentrates on the most important elements early on in the design process, one should be aware that it inherently imposes an evaluation and that others may have different opinions on what is regarded as "important". A fourth plan provides a discussion and interpretation of the first three plans:

4. CONSERVATION PLAN

At this stage, evaluation is explicitly desirable and the plan should serve as a basis for further discussion. It is the architect's task to identify and map all aspects which determine, influence or otherwise restrict the later design process. The conservation plan draws upon the three plans above and evaluates the findings. The evaluation should be marked clearly and unambiguously: it is better to state openly from the outset which elements one regards as less important rather than to have to enter into heated debate later on during the building process. The conservation plan usually contains a categorisation of elements according to their value, e.g. "interventions possible", "interventions only in particular conditions", and "must be retained". Categorisations should be made both for the BUILDING SHELL AND STRUCTURE as well as for FITTINGS AND FIXTURES.

This plan provides a breakdown of the most important findings and the condition of the building and weighs up positive observations and deficiencies. The reasoning behind the evaluation should be described in the text. The measured drawings, the investigations undertaken and the final analysis of strengths and weaknesses provide the architect with all the information necessary for the later development of a design. The challenge for the architect is to maintain an overview of the many individual aspects that need to be considered and to develop an overall planning strategy that takes these into account.

In some cases, the assessment of the preliminary investigations may lead to the painful conclusion that the intended future use or envisaged building measures are not compatible with the existing building. An attempt to implement plans regardless of incompatibilities very often results in large scale damage to the original building substance and therefore also devalues the property itself. From an economic point of view, it is advisable to find a more suitable use for the old building and an alternative housing for the incompatible function.

Further reading

As an introduction to measured building surveying we recommend CRAMER 1993, ECKSTEIN and KLEIN. ECKERT and FRANZ provide details of working with archives. MATTHEWS is a standard reference work on modern surveying and further surveying issues are discussed by WANGERIN; digital techniques are illustrated by WIEDEMANN as well as in the anthologies by WEFERLING et al. RODWELL describes his personal experience in the field. An overview of the application of modern photogrammetry is given by ALMAGRO.

GROSSMANN 1993, TUSSENBROEK and SCHULLER provide a systematic introduction to historical research; WOOD illustrates these with many examples and BEDAL outlines surveying approaches to residential building research. The basic standards of archaeological documentation are described by GERKAN 1930, and H. SCHMIDT and DOCCI describe the history of the methods employed. Dendrochronology is described by SCHWEINGRUBER, EISSING and SCHÖFBECK. The use of thermography in surveying existing buildings is described by CRAMER 1981.

The fundamental principles of restoration are described in BRANDI and SCHÄDLER-SAUB. RENFREW and FEHRING describe the basic archaeological principles. The documentation of building measures for historic buildings is described by DE JONGE/VAN BALEN, PETZET/MADER, THOMAS and MADER. The room log was developed by W. SCHMIDT. Simplified approaches to surveying are described by ARENDT, KASTNER, BAUEN IM BESTAND and KLEMISCH. GÄNSSMANTEL/GEBURTIG/SCHAU illustrate how modern building documentation methods have progressed beyond the traditional graphical building survey to serve the purposes of facility management.

DESIGN STRATEGIES

Every place is open to innovation as long as there is innovation. Giorgio Piccinato

Developing architectural designs in the context of an existing building is no less demanding than creating a design for a new building. The development of an effective and functional building plan, a coherent design concept and the coordinated choice of materials is just as important for old buildings as it is for new. In the process of converting an old building, the architect should be aware that a consistent approach is required in order to avoid the large number of bespoke situations from leading to a variety of disconnected, individual solutions. At the same time, the existing building should not be subordinated to an artificial conceptual straitjacket, nor be disfigured to the extent that it is no longer recognisable – effectively resulting in the loss of its qualities. The tension between the specific individual characteristics of a building that has evolved over time, and the desire to achieve a coherent and consistent design concept, is what characterises architectural design in the context of existing buildings. A good design concept not only exploits the qualities and possibilities a building offers; it contributes to contemporary architectural discourse and also upholds sustainability far beyond the guarantee period. And even more than in the design of a new building, the quality of workmanship is decisive for the quality of the final result.

Modernisation of a façade from the turn of the century in Milan, Italy (Giovanni Muzio, 1923). The unusual solution earned it the nickname "Ca' brutta".

The Marienkirche in Müncheberg, Germany (Klaus Bock, 1999). The insertion of a library into part of the church interior occupies a space no longer required for the smaller church congregation.

The Alte Pinakothek in Munich, Germany, reconstructed using the rubble in a simplified form. An iconic work of architecture in existing fabric (Hans Döllgast, 1956).

Designing with history

The challenge of using an old, often damaged, building as the basis and context for a new and ambitious design project was first taken up in modern times by architects rebuilding cities after the ravages of the Second World War. Projects such as Hans Döllgast's creative reconstruction of the Alte Pinakothek in Munich or Rudolf Schwarz's work in Cologne are justly famous and still exemplary today. Although many comparable projects were undertaken at the time, none of the protagonists developed a theoretical approach to their design and much of their experience was lost after the main wave of reconstruction had been completed. In the 1960s and early 1970s, Carlo Scarpa remained as the solitary protagonist involved in architecture in a historical context, with his exacting and meticulously detailed designs strongly informed by the tradition of arts and crafts. His approach to presenting historical fragments and of characterising individual formal values was inspiring to others, and a small school of like-minded architects formed including Karljosef Schattner, Guido Canali and Massimo Carmassi. Standing firmly in the Modernist tradition, they champion its principle credo to break with the past and to innovate without compromise, but in the context of the historical environment. They clearly and consciously demarcate the boundary between the old and new in form and in principle: the old appears as a relic of a no longer comprehensible but nevertheless dignified past; the new building or

The reconstruction of the Gürzenich in Cologne, Germany, a leading example of a self-assured and yet historical reconstruction after the war (Rudolf Schwarz, 1958).

Reconstruction using old building materials and a composition of historic remnants from war rubble in Wroclaw, Poland.

A thematic interpretation of the castle using concrete and showing little regard for the existing building fabric: Castelgrande in Bellinzona, Switzerland (Aurelio Galfetti, 1989).

building element distinguishes itself through its own materiality, employing new structural concepts and design approaches as an expression of the present, and of the future emerging out of it. Such architecture conveys a message, as if declaring the position of mankind as time passes.

The architectural expression and style of each of these architects is nevertheless highly individual. Out of a primarily analytical approach, often involving fragmentation strategies, different styles have arisen: Scarpa developed a highly poetic architecture; other architects have employed the strongly didactic approach of a "window on the past" in which an opening in the modern building frames a view of a section of the original historic building substance; still others have adopted an ironic architectural language, such as Schattner's "falsifications" of historic finds. In the 1980s some architects began to explicitly emphasise the value of history in its own right. Carmassi, for example, employs creative processes of analysis and fragmentation to enhance the quality of the original. In a carefully orchestrated process of assembly and reframing, residual colouring is enhanced or comparatively insignificant historic building elements appear ennobled when set against a background of facing brickwork. Through their carefully crafted appearance, these buildings refer to the special quality inherent in historic architecture.

Renewed interest in the urban and the historical built environment brought about a revival of renovation and conversion work in the 1970s. Of particular interest from a theoretical point of view is a greater readiness to draw inspiration from the historic building fabric and to develop something new out of its specific characteristics. A careful analysis of the existing context is used to define the structures within which sensitive modernisation measures and new designs can be developed.

This kind of analysis based upon an examination of the *genius loci*, the spirit of a place, can be harnessed in other ways for the design process as well. In his commentary to Rowe and Slutzky's book *Transparency*, Bernhard

Hoesli adopts a method for the critical analysis for interpreting modern architecture and applies it directly to design in the historical built context and within the European city. Drawing upon the notion of transparency, he reveals structures and geometric proportions in the existing built context, which are then used as a basis for design. In a manner not dissimilar to the traditional principles of proportion, he reduced both the existing context as well as the new design to a series of simple geometric patterns, deriving a common basis for both new and old. Here the new is not simply created as a contrast to the old, but as a continuation of its pattern of development. In this way, a new building, for instance an infill in a row of historic buildings, is structurally as well as historically related to the place, even if in appearance it looks quite different. This approach can be as simple as continuing the eaves line and pattern of window openings; it can draw upon particular formal characteristics or it can choose to highlight an individual aspect of the history of a place. Several designs by Peter Eisenman and Daniel Libeskind adopt this latter approach. For example, in their respective projects in Berlin, an analysis of particular aspects of the context – the residences of specific individuals or the historical arrangement of the urban surroundings – provides data points and reference lines, with the resulting meshwork of lines serving as generators for the design in plan and elevation. The appeal of such methods is in the understanding of the transformations of the built environment as a continuum in which the building's design is situated. The new building is conceived as a further layer added to the palimpsest of traces from previous times. Specific historic occurrences are deemed as being fundamentally important and expressed through the design. The user or visitor is made aware of the continuum in which he or she stands. This notion that beneath the surface, basic patterns and characteristics persist, a kind of baseline upon which the fashions and styles play their melodies, is fundamental to a specifically European comprehension of the city.

Last but not least, as Alison and Peter Smithson have shown with their *"As found"* approach, published in 1990, every urban situation and every building has its own specific and embedded value – it is the designer's task to perceive and discover it. By drawing on this intrinsic value, even a simple building can assume new meaning and a new future with comparatively little effort. The building becomes an *objet trouvé*, an inadvertent work of art that touches and engages us with its apparent foreignness and seemingly unintelligible message from the past.

As Found – every house has the potential for alteration: a new layer around an old house in rural surroundings.

When one examines current architectural projects, it appears that many architects have found a clear concept for developing designs in the context of existing buildings. Post-modern complexity, a revival in the appreciation of character and uniqueness and a renewed interest in the materiality of architecture are closely intertwined with the natural development of the built environment.

In recent years a fourth approach has gained increasing importance: the integration of the new as a conscious continuation of the existing. This approach regards the contrasting of old and new as visual and functional fragmentation at the cost of architectural unity. Street scenes characterised by a series of excessively strong architectural statements are regarded as undesirable, possibly because after the initial attraction has waned, the danger is that one is left with a series of empty clichés. The wish for greater unity and harmony in the built environment goes hand in hand with a latent desire to smoothen the transition of history. Against this background, design in the context of the built environment becomes a statement of the architect's attitude towards history.

Does design within the built environment differ formally from that for new buildings? The answer is, of course, no. Many of the design strategies, concepts and possibilities described in this chapter have originated in new buildings and have later been applied to conversion projects; others have made the opposite transition. For example, MECANOO's and Erick van Egeraats's concept for a conference room, suspended in the courtyard of a turn-of-the-century town house, is in principle identical to a similar formal solution by Frank Gehry in the entirely new building for the DG Bank in Berlin. The exposed cable-runs fixed to the facing concrete of the Kunsthal in Rotterdam, planned by Rem Koolhaas and built in 1993, also represent an ideal and sustainable solution for an old building. And ever since the Centre Pompidou in Paris, the arrangement of circulation and services on the outside of a building has also become well-known for new buildings. Similarly, the variety of different forms seen in buildings that have undergone many changes in their lifetime has become inspirational for a generation of post-modern designers. Hans Hollein's "Haas-Haus" in Vienna exhibits this approach clearly. Similarly, Charles W. Moore's project for the Piazza d'Italia in New Orleans, the dislodged stones in James Stirling's Staatsgalerie in Stuttgart or the provocative projects by SITE in the United States are further examples of modern architecture that play with the theme of historical fragments. Even the most straightforward continuation of historical forms into the present, a long unbroken tradition in the English speaking world and France, so vehemently opposed by international modernism in the 1920s, has seen a revival in the architecture of Hans Kollhoff or Paul Kahlfeldt. Why shouldn't such approaches to new building apply equally well for working with existing buildings?

Disposition

Every design for an existing building changes it in some way. The change is intentional and accepted as such. In this respect, designs for existing buildings differ fundamentally from the special case of conservation work, which regards all change with a degree of scepticism. However, the fact that alterations will be necessary and also desirable should not serve as an excuse to effect changes that significantly impact on the identity of the existing building. The gutting of a building in order to achieve an optimal spatial arrangement effectively eradicates the building's identity and the ability to use its existing structure in any other way in the future. The consideration of an existing building only in terms of its external appearance and urban presence ignores its cultural and artistic values and shows disregard for both cost-effectiveness and sustainability. The decision to gut or demolish a building is almost always the result of inflexibility and a lack of willingness to engage cre-

The complete gutting of the salt museum in Hallein, Austria: a reductionist approach leaving only the external walls standing and discarding the social, historic and aesthetic value of the existing building (Heinz Tesar, 1995).

atively with the building as found. Through the selection of an appropriate use, where necessary with auxiliary buildings for special requirements, it is possible to find an architecturally appealing and functionally effective solution for almost any historic building.

Definition of appropriate function

A fundamental aspect of the quality of a design is determined at the very outset of the planning and design process: to what degree is the envisaged use compatible with the existing building? A continuation of the existing function generally results in the least conflict. It is easier to plan new flats in an existing residential building or offices in a former factory than to convert a multi-storey car park to owner-occupied flats or open-plan offices to urban residences. The notion that the best use of an old building is the continuation of its existing function was first explicitly formulated as part of the 1964 Venice Charter. However, the architect should not view this dogmatically. Sometimes the mark of a successful project is the tension between the expected use, i.e. what the original building conveys, and a completely different, new function that has been cleverly fitted into it. It should, however, also be self-evident that a radical CHANGE OF USE will almost always involve major and costly conversion works to the building substance and may often cause a series of additional problems. The conversion of fifteen town houses to a hotel will necessitate major changes to the access and circulation; likewise, the introduction of flats into a former church will involve significant new structural works. Not every client can be convinced of the necessity of such expensive solutions. A design for an existing building will be most successful when it avoids unnecessary problems. For this reason, the existing building structure should inform the future use of the building, and not vice versa. This is not simply a matter of quantifiable material advantages but also of the nature of the building: the "aura" of a historic building informs its later use. It is

Smaller room partitions beneath a large Baroque stuccoed ceiling. The new walls maintain a distance to the existing building, a technique previously used by Le Corbusier in the 1920s. Markt 33, Braunau, Austria (Laurids Ortner, 1994).

Renovation as a fragment

Municipal archives in the Church of San Agostin, 2004
Valladolid, Spain
Client: City of Valladolid
Architect: Primitivo Gonzalez and Gabriel Gallegos

The condition of the church before conversion works began.

In the first half of the 20th century, the baroque church had already decayed considerably and the monastery had had to be demolished. After extensive archaeological investigations had been undertaken, the conversion of the building for use as the municipal archives began. The aim was to maintain the ruin as a legible fragment: the collapsed vaulted ceiling is capped by a modern wooden ceiling, the stumps of broken walls are plainly whitewashed, and the uneven old walls contrast with the smooth insertions made of wood and metal. Remains of the Romanesque cloister arcade are presented out of context on a raised "rack" for all to see.

Archaeological dig in the nave of the church.

General view showing the raised display of the remains of the cloister.

The old irregular walls contrast with the smooth modern insertions.

The interior of the church houses the reading room.

no coincidence that most former churches are re-used for cultural purposes such as museums, public function rooms or concert halls and not for commercial or residential purposes. An appropriate choice of function will also be most readily accepted, and therefore contributes to the long-term sustainability of the conversion works.

Sensitive interventions
The building plan, the distribution of rooms and the circulation in an old building very often differs from the typical arrangement that would be used when planning a new building. Room heights may be too high or too low and the proportions, shapes and succession of rooms in old buildings were generally determined by the evolution of the building, the pattern of use and the technical limitations of the time. Very often the historic pattern of circulation and access is at odds with contemporary requirements: the Baroque enfilade of rooms was the height of fashion in its day, but today it results in rooms trapped behind other rooms; narrow staircases were normal up until the 19th century, today they are unacceptable. Grant funding sometimes stipulates particular room sizes for particular functions. The temptation to alter the existing plan through the removal and re-introduction of walls so that it fulfils the requirements is understandable. It goes

The concert hall as an autonomous construction inserted into the Beurs van Berlage Commodities Exchange in Amsterdam built by Berlage in 1904 (Zaanen/Spanjers, 1990).

A stair that supports the house

Tabourettli Theatre in the old Spalenhof, 1988
Basel, Switzerland
Client: private
Architect: Santiago Calatrava

On the upper floor of a late medieval house in the old town of Basel, a hall was to be converted for small-scale events. The atmosphere of the surroundings is characterised by its history. The adaptation of the rooms made improvements to the circulation and the structure necessary. The design solution combines both in a single structure: the stair construction transfers the load of the upper storey to the foundation. The flamboyant design of the stair is mirrored in the treatment of the ceiling and furnishings.

The elegant sweeping stair leading to the theatre.

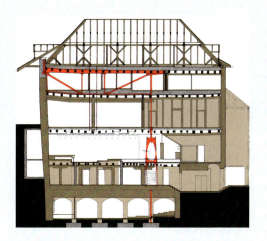

Section showing the extent of building measures. The new structures are marked in red.

The modern support structure designed by Santiago Calatrava (model photo).

Sketch illustrating the construction principle.

without saying that such design strategies not only impact significantly on the identity of the old building but also entail major alterations to the building structure with all their associated technical and structural consequences. The most sensitive option therefore is to maintain the basic room structure as dictated by the load-bearing structure. Partitioning walls that are non-load-bearing, whether part of the original building or added at a later date, can be removed without any consequences for the building structure, although it is important to bear in mind that their removal may impact on valuable fixtures or finishes.

These considerations do not mean that changes to the building plan should be rejected outright, but at the same time at it makes little sense to shift a wall by a few centimetres to fulfil grant stipulations or to slightly raise a ceiling to conform to minimum room-heights for building regulations. In both cases it can be more viable to leave large areas of the existing building as they are and to compensate for the disadvantages with more radical interventions in other areas of the building. For instance, one could completely remove only some of the too low ceilings; where a part of the building is badly damaged, this section could be completely rebuilt with a different building plan; a tiny bedroom could be compensated for with a spacious and airy living room in the roof space; dark access corridors can be made more attractive through naturally lit seating areas at each end. Old buildings only rarely correspond to schematic standards, and in the same way as relaxations to regulations are gradually being granted in recognition of this, the planning approach should focus rather on the strengths that a building has. The aim of planning should on the one hand be to maintain and build upon the identity of the building in its structure and plan, and on the other to improve its usability and make it more attractive through well-chosen, selected interventions.

Auxiliary constructions

Over the past decades, our expectations of comfort levels as well as technical building standards have changed radically. As a result, very few old buildings are able to fulfil contemporary expectations without some degree of modernisation. Typically each deficit is investigated and remedied in turn, however a more holistic approach can prove more effective: by locating those functions that require more serious changes in order to fulfil modern-day requirements in auxiliary constructions, for instance in a part of the building that will need to be rebuilt anyway or as part of an extension, it is possible to minimise the conflict between historic building substance and modern-day requirements. Even in cases where new building sections are not imperative it can still be worthwhile to consider locating complex requirements in auxiliary constructions, for instance in the form of a new extension or external construction. One of the most common problems is the provision of lifts and disabled access in historic buildings. In most cases, existing stair-

Improved circulation in the National Portrait Gallery in London made by inserting a new entrance and stair into a small courtyard (Jeremy Dixon and Edward Jones, 2000).

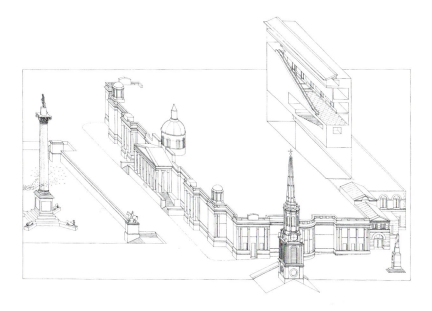

An additional storey clad in perforated steel sheeting is added to an unassuming residence in the narrow streets of Eichstätt, Germany.

In London a new roof structure is hoisted onto an old building like a big piece of furniture. Its form earned it the name "White Cube" (MRJ Rundell & Associates, 2002).

cases and stairs do not fulfil fire safety regulations and their dimensions and steepness often conflict with building regulations. The first step is to discuss whether a relaxation of the regulations will be permitted for the old building substance. However, even if consent is granted, the question of how to provide disabled access remains. And even if the old staircase was removed in its entirety and replaced with a new construction, a lift may still not fit into the available space.

An alternative strategy is often simpler: by locating the new access requirements in a custom-built external auxiliary construction, the existing building fabric can be preserved. As a new construction, it can be built to conform to building regulations without impacting on the existing building.

Conference room suspended over a courtyard

Bank in a 19th century building, 1997
Budapest, Hungary
Client: ING-Bank
Architect: MECANOO, Erick van Egeraat

The 19th century building is well suited for use as offices but the integration of larger rooms is only possible by making major alterations. The design concept tackles this problem by locating a large new structure above the internal courtyard, in this way turning it into an atrium. The structural capacity of the existing building is sufficient to bear the weight of the new structure which in terms of design is independent of the old building. Its amorphous, organic form as well as its materials and surface finish contrast with the surrounding building.

Glass roof and circulation around the conference room.

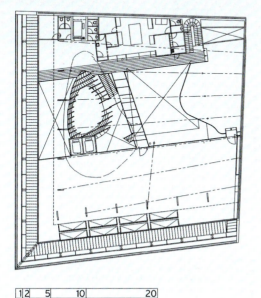

Floor plan at the level of the conference room.

The freeform conference room suspended over the courtyard.

The new construction may be built as a subordinate extension of the existing building or as a completely separate construction placed alongside but apart from it. A common strategy is to insert new circulation requirements in courtyards or adjacent areas of the plot. The roofing over of previously open courtyards, although often involving complex solutions for fire regulations, ventilation and lighting, can create new and attractive spatial constellations.

The same principle can likewise be applied for other technical requirements that are difficult to incorporate in the existing construction. For example, before attempting to integrate new sanitary installations into an old half-timbered house, or to create large rooms by demolishing separating walls, it may make more sense to locate these in an extension, perhaps in connection with a new external access construction.

The addition of a further storey is another means of achieving similar aims. Buildings erected before the First World War in particular are often solid enough to bear the load of one or two additional storeys. This allows greater exploitation of the existing plot as well as the creation of spaces that can serve new purposes. It makes sense to locate larger rooms in the new stories. This approach is dependent not only on the load-bearing capacity of the foundations and walls, but also determined by fire regulations and possibly by local development or conservation plans.

Design strategies

The design concept is informed by the existing building, the condition it is in and the overall project aims. As the decision for a particular design strategy will shape the subsequent steps in the design process, it is important to discuss the different options early on with all who are involved in the project. By clarifying the direction from the outset, the architect will have the necessary backing and freedom to elaborate a design proposal. The design task will vary depending upon which values one chooses to view as more or less important, and without a clear concept a design may end up as an unsatisfactory mixture of different conceptual approaches.

A central question when deciding between different design concepts is the extent and degree of interventions and alterations they entail. The range of options varies from simple corrective maintenance, to upgrading and modernisation works to deliberate alteration and extension. A final option is the possibility to demolish and replace the existing building. It is safe to say that the more extensive the alterations will be, the greater the cost – and vice versa. In principle, the decision to undertake major alterations and incur high costs is not necessarily bad, however, the architect will need to be able to justify the decision, and explain the reasoning behind the chosen concept, its implications and the expected results.

In reality, a particular design strategy is chosen less often than one might expect on the basis of a conscious analysis of the condition and pattern of damage. All too often, unclear expectations concerning the values of the building and vague hopes of improving the value of the property determine the choice of strategy, without the implications of decisions being properly considered. For this reason, it is particularly important to think through the eventual consequences of a particular design strategy, right from the very outset.

Corrective maintenance

The greatest immaterial asset of a historic building is its age. Our appreciation of its very existence and the fact that it has survived for so long, often exhibiting wear and tear, provides us with a window onto the past and anchors the building in the course of time. The attempt to hold off or even negate the effects of aging robs it of its dignity and identity. The buildings of the past, as John Ruskin writes in *The Seven Lamps of Architecture*, *"... are not ours. They belong partly to those who built them, and partly to all*

The garden elevation after completion of renovation works.

"Rinsing" salts from the brickwork through continuous irrigation with a normal garden sprinkler system.

The condition as found before renovation work began.

Adaptation by repair

Renovation of a private residence, 2006
Venice, Italy
Client: City of Venice
Architect: Piana and Schubert

In the renovation of the unprepossessing house on the edge of Venice, special emphasis was given to maintaining its varied historical identity. The deformations and settlement in parts of the building were not changed; instead the repairs were adapted to fit the prevailing conditions. Traditional techniques and workmanship were employed for the renovation works and the overall result is restrained and calm. The division of the former private residence into four residential units adapts the building to contemporary requirements.

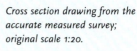

Cross section drawing from the accurate measured survey; original scale 1:20.

The renovated and repaired terrazzo floor and smooth plastered walls after completion of renovation works.

Saved from collapse

Structural stabilisation and renovation
of a medieval house, 2005
Bamberg, Germany
Client: private
Planning: Hans Reuter

Over several hundred years, the medieval house next to the Obere Brücke in the centre of Bamberg had gradually tilted more and more towards the water until it was feared it would collapse. An accurate measured survey was undertaken documenting the distortion of the building and all defects. Based upon this survey, a structural solution was drawn up that uses a steel framework to take up the load and convey it to a strengthened foundation. The steel framework was welded in the workshop and inserted and screwed together on site. Other interventions to stabilise the structure did not need to be undertaken.

The crooked three-storey house on the water's edge.

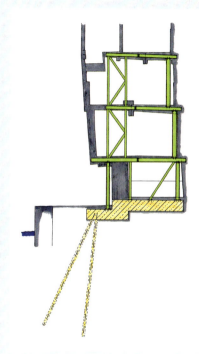

Drawing detailing the structural stabilisation.

An accurate measured drawing documents the degree of distortion of the building.

A new steel framework stops the building from toppling.

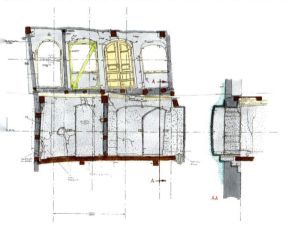

the generations of mankind who are to follow us." He argues that a restoration destroys the most valuable assets of a historic building. ALLOWING A BUILDING TO AGE consequently is not only an inexpensive option; it also maintains its value. If this approach is taken, a design may not actually result in any noticeable works, and for some architects this may seem insufficient; it requires a degree of self-assurance to allow a building to speak of its age without feeling the need to introduce contemporary elements.

A sensitive architect will always consider if and where the effects of aging should best be accepted as they are, as well as to what degree the aging process can be slowed down through appropriate MAINTENANCE without affecting the impression of age that lends the building its identity.

Where maintenance is not sufficient, sensitive REPAIRS can secure the long-term future of a building. In this context, repairs encompass the correction of defects in the existing building fabric which do not require extensive material replacement, or changes to the overall structure. As they are counted as part of the general maintenance costs, they should always be inexpensive. Repairs should always use the same materials and techniques as the original construction. Where contractors are not familiar with traditional craftsmen's skills, the risk of unintentional damage can be high. The phrase "repairs to the repairs" (familiar from recent publications) testifies to the problems associated with utilising contemporary and inappropriate techniques for the refurbishment of historic buildings.

Maintenance works can include RESTORATION, the purpose of which is to stabilise and improve the condition of damaged fabric, as well as CONSERVATION, which simply stabilises the condition as found. Both options can clearly be attributed to the field of building conservation, but this does not preclude them from being appropriate in other contexts. Many techniques from the field of building conservation not only have proven effectiveness, but are also inexpensive and ecologically sound, and therefore eminently suitable for use when dealing with historic buildings. As such, the repair of damaged building fabric using conservation techniques is not merely a possible option, but often a sensible one.

Modernisation

The improvement of a building for contemporary purposes, whether it is known as adaptation, upgrading, rehabilitation, renovation or modernisation, is a natural part of the building's life cycle. Standards change and existing buildings will continually be adapted to fit current expectations. The skilful adaptation of a building to fulfil new requirements is not only a challenging design task for an architect, but is also a practically inexhaustible field of work. Nevertheless, many architects do not find it easy to place themselves in the "servitude" of an old building, and "modernisation" is often regarded as the unloved cousin of "true" architecture – even the word itself has a technocratic and uncreative ring to it.

In contrast to this, the innovative potential of modernisation has been exploited successfully by interior designers, who have explored its creative possibilities for many years. This includes not only sensitive responses to the historic and spatial context through appropriate fittings and furnishings but also methods that bring out the haptic or visual qualities of historic materials. In the retail sector, historic fragments have become a much-loved and almost indispensable element of shop design, and the "raw finish" of old walls adorns many trendy fashion shops, though more so for its atmospheric effect than any actual historic value.

In everyday terms, modernisation can often simply mean the improvement of the overall appearance of the building through the redesign or repainting of the façade. For the architect in the first instance it entails adapting the existing building to the requirements of modern infrastructure. Only in

The old walls of the Casa Muti in Pisa, Italy, form a dramatic contrast to the modern insertion (Massimo Carmassi, 1991).

The exposed Roman walls as an "atmospheric" background for the up-market range of goods (Split, Croatia).

A new bridge marks the entrance to the Palazzo.

Artful addition

Adaptation of a Palazzo to a museum, 1963
Venice, Italy
Client: Fondazione Querini-Stampalia
Architect: Carlo Scarpa

The architect was asked to develop a solution for the ground floor rooms and garden which were subject to flooding. Scarpa began by raising the level of circulation in the building through the design of an intricate and detailed insertion that echoes, among other things, the entrance channels for boats in Venice. His artful and elaborate additions contrast with the rough surfaces of the exposed brickwork walls. Technical installations are not hidden away but treated as independent volumes. Similarly, other deficiencies are not solved by replacing elements but by employing additive measures. The craftsmanship of the new additions connects the new with the old.

Design sketch for the repair of a worn stair.

The stair after conversion measures.

Raised circulation routes, new technical installations housed in free-standing elements.

rare cases will it be possible to continue using the existing heating, sanitary and electrical installations. The first question is therefore which strategy is most appropriate for the renewal of technical services. In addition to considering that old buildings will generally necessitate more detailed and complex coordination with services engineers, the architect will also need to examine whether the existing routing of services is sensible. The renewal of the existing services as routed in the building will often entail a considerable amount of destruction, regardless of how carefully the measures have been planned – the plaster along all cables will have to be removed and openings made in floors and walls for water, waste and heating installations. In order to reduce this damage, as well as the subsequent repairs entailed, it may make more sense to change the routing or to surface-mount new cabling rather than to embed it in plaster. In many old buildings built before the 1950s, unused chimney flues are ideally suited for vertical installation risers. The architect will only need to ensure that sanitary and electrical installations are kept separate and that fire breaks are provided to stop the spread of fire between floors. For the horizontal routing of electrical installations and heating pipes on each floor, a large number of acceptable solutions are now available.

In addition to the renewal of electrical and heating installations, modernisation measures usually also result in significant changes to kitchens and bathrooms. The variety of sanitary facilities in a modern bathroom necessitates a more differentiated distribution of services, and the risk of leakages and spillages is the main problem, particularly for timber floors. The installation of enclosed

The technical installations in this loft in Madrid, Spain, are surface-mounted and can be repaired and replaced easily (Manuel Serrano, 2005).

WC-container in the 2nd floor of a former warehouse in Nijmegen, Holland, now converted for use as a gallery. An independent insertion for independent sanitary installations (Diederen and Dirrix, 1997).

The outside lift provides comfortable access without impacting on the building fabric in Schaffhausen, Switzerland.

and stable containers with specifically designed transfer points for water installations reduces the risk and extent of leaks.

When reorganising floor plans, changes should avoid alterations to the load-bearing system wherever possible. For example, cramped conditions can be relieved by removing partitioning walls that were introduced in many buildings after the war to alleviate the housing shortage. The reorganisation of circulation and entry, for instance through the addition of a porch, can upgrade an entrance situation. Combining two small flats in a worker's housing estate makes it possible to provide attractive living conditions for families. The addition of a self-supporting balcony construction to the outside of a building makes the flats within more attractive and increases the floor area.

Last but not least, modernisation also includes upgrading the energy-efficiency of a building. Modern requirements almost always necessitate that heat loss is reduced wherever possible whilst at the same time improving the indoor environment. The heavy thermal mass of the load-bearing walls of historic buildings is an often largely underused potential. At the same time, historic building materials can react sensitively to ill-conceived upgrading measures, for example inadequate moisture diffusion as a result of excessive insulation. Rather than viewing this susceptibility as a disadvantage, one can instead regard it as a kind of inbuilt early warning mechanism, signalling deficiencies before harm occurs to the inhabitants or users.

Where a building undergoes a change of use, the existing load-bearing structure may not be sufficient for the new load. The design of strengthening measures which not only serve their purpose but also harmonise with the existing building and its appearance is a particularly demanding design task. Structural engineers have developed a variety of cost-effective techniques for catering for increased load requirements whilst avoiding impacting on the fabric and identity of the building.

More recently, modernisation measures have also included the removal of hazardous and toxic building materials to ensure the long-term sustainable and healthy use of a building.

Adaptation

The adaptation of existing buildings to ensure their continued use is a central aspect of architectural design in existing built contexts. Although there is some overlap with modernisation, adaptation is generally characterised by a change in the character of the building as a result of a change of use or fundamental building works. Adaptation also means creative transformation, and the input of the architect is usually visible to a greater or lesser extent alongside the historic characteristics of the existing building. The basic options for adaptations are relatively limited: the subdivision of a building by introducing new walls and floors adapts it to new uses without changing its general form; the conversion of a building involves making sometimes significant changes to the building substance but respects its overall volume; the extension adds new functions and built elements to an existing building; and finally, the method of combination unifies several buildings into a single unit.

The simplest way to ensure the continued development of a building is through a change of use. For many kinds of buildings, changes of use take place all the time without requiring significant alterations to the building. For example, a change of use from residential or commercial premises to offices is relatively straightforward. Even more fundamental changes of use or the extension of usable space can often be realised without major or costly interventions, and without sacrificing the building's identity.

Large volume and large floor area: The church of St. Maximin in Trier, Germany, is converted into a sports hall (Gottfried Böhm and Dieter Baumewerd, 1995).

In times of property market slump or long decision-making processes, an INTERIM TEMPORARY USAGE can ensure the continued use of a building, as well as continued income, without the need for large-scale investment.

The SUBDIVISION of large and spacious buildings using architectural means (as opposed to interior design) has numerous historic precedents. After the Reformation in the 16th century, and later again during secularisation as well as after the Second

Complete conversion: Classical statues stand between machines of the ACEA electricity works, both carefully restored, in Rome (ACEA, Comune di Roma, 1997).

Conversion as refurnishing: The Interbau Pavilion in Berlin, built in 1957 by Fehling and Gogel, now serves as a fast food restaurant (Petra and Paul Kahlfeldt, 2006).

Temporary use of the doomed Palast der Republik in Berlin (Urban Catalysts/raumlabor berlin, 2005).

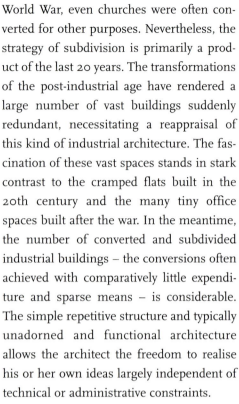

World War, even churches were often converted for other purposes. Nevertheless, the strategy of subdivision is primarily a product of the last 20 years. The transformations of the post-industrial age have rendered a large number of vast buildings suddenly redundant, necessitating a reappraisal of this kind of industrial architecture. The fascination of these vast spaces stands in stark contrast to the cramped flats built in the 20th century and the many tiny office spaces built after the war. In the meantime, the number of converted and subdivided industrial buildings – the conversions often achieved with comparatively little expenditure and sparse means – is considerable. The simple repetitive structure and typically unadorned and functional architecture allows the architect the freedom to realise his or her own ideas largely independent of technical or administrative constraints.

Numerous architects have tackled the problem of inserting new uses into large existing spaces by taking a HOUSE-IN-HOUSE approach, in which the new use is more or

Loft in a shed

Living in an industrial building, 2005
Madrid, Spain
Client: private
Architect: Manuel Serrano

The conversion of an architecturally insignificant industrial building in Madrid's "Loftown" retains the envelope of the original industrial building and inserts a mezzanine into the high space, connecting it to the floor below with a constructivist stair. All technical installations are surface-mounted on the exposed walls. If necessary they, as well as the other insertions, can be removed or repaired with ease. The smooth finish of the new insertions contrasts with the irregular surfaces of the old building.

The stairwell with constructivist-inspired staircase and surface-mounted technical installations.

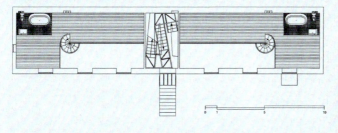

Plan.

Furniture on rollers emphasises the functional flexibility of the insertions.

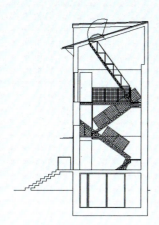

Section.

The bathroom is the only enclosed room on the gallery.

Exterior view of the new structure and the converted industrial building.

Transforming obsolete industrial buildings

Conversion and extension of an industrial building, 2004
Göttelborn, Germany
Client: Industriekultur Saar GmbH
Architect: Augustin und Frank

Both of the industrial buildings from the 1960s have no inherent historic value. Before the pithead was closed, they served as auxiliary structures for the mining works. Their conversion for administrative and public functions makes use of the intact construction and solves the lack of thermal insulation through the addition of an innovative second skin. The design is completed by high-quality interior work in both buildings that is appropriate to their industrial character. A new structure provides guest accommodation. The overall appearance is characterised by industrial materials.

Both industrial buildings before conversion.

Interior view after conversion.   *Interior view after conversion.*

Section through the existing building and new addition showing the new energy-efficient building skin.

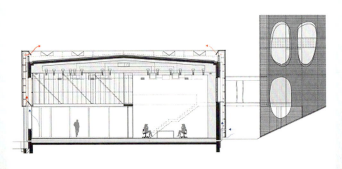

less independent of the existing construction. Although from a historic point of view this approach is admirable, difficulties arise where individual spaces within the building need to be attached to the external façade for light and ventilation. The approach is most successful where the existing space is large enough for new uses to be inserted as freestanding objects. It is no surprise that the conversion of many churches follows this basic principle.

In the history of architecture there is a long tradition of the COMPLETION of buildings at a later date. The tradition of building where others had left off in the past began long before the 19th century practice of completing the towers of gothic cathedrals, for example. Buildings have often been built on or out of the ruins of their predecessors. After the

The almost untouched envelope of a factory building in Shanghai, China, now houses offices (Ma Weidong and Teng Kunyen, 1997).

Later use of an unfinished construction from 1960 for the Winter Olympics in Turin, Italy, as an ice rink (Gae Aulenti, 2006).

The climbing labyrinth in the "MACHmit! Children's Museum" in Berlin – a large piece of furniture inserted into a church (Klaus Block, 2003).

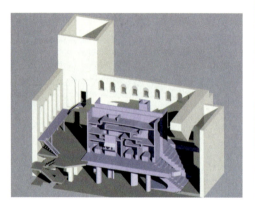

The garages for vintage cars in the Meilenwerk, Berlin, are an independent construction over several storeys within the former tram depot (Dinse, Feest, Zurl, 2003).

Small office cubicles for the university administration in the large banquet hall of the Orangerie in Eichstätt, Germany (Karljosef Schattner, 1974).

Furnishing a church

Hotel in a monastery church, 2005
Maastricht, Netherlands
Client: Stichting Monumentaal Erfgoed Limburg
Architect: Rob Brouwers, SATIJNplus Architecten

The former Deutschorden monastery was secularised in the 19th century and was used for a number of different purposes before being converted into a hotel. The design concept leaves the monks' accommodation largely unchanged and, excepting the modern furnishings, uses the existing structure without significant modifications for the hotel rooms. The church itself houses the reception area, offices, lounge, bar and restaurant. All of these functions are accommodated in two-storey constructions that, like pieces of furniture, are placed within the church as freestanding objects without touching the walls. The irregularity of the gothic building contrasts with the smoothness of the new insertions and the transparency of the glazed lift. The experience of entering the building is heightened by a sculptural funnel-like construction made of polished copper.

The restaurant, a freestanding object placed within the church.

The new insertion contrasts deliberately with its historic surroundings.

The entrance as a piece of sculpture.

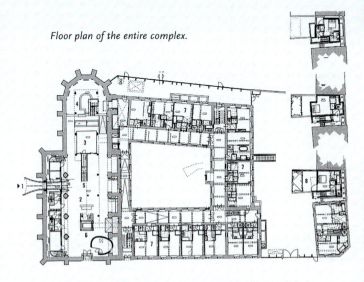

Floor plan of the entire complex.

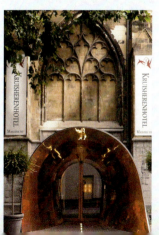

Second World War, the period of rebuilding is characterised by numerous creative attempts at finishing incomplete remains. The principle of continuing the existing structure of the building but in a simplified form, as exemplified by Hans Döllgast's legendary reconstruction of the Alte Pinakothek in Munich, remains as valid as ever: The spatial form, proportion and building structure is maintained, but surface modulations and decoration is either reproduced in a simplified form or simply omitted. The highly original solutions developed by Gottfried Böhm for Saarbrucken Castle in the 1980s or by Chipperfield/Harrap for the Neues Museum in Berlin (early 21st century) show that two generations later this approach has lost none of its appeal. Catastrophes, such as those resulting from fire, will continue to challenge architects to find a respectful balance between qualitative conservation and modern additions. A 1:1 RECONSTRUCTION of the past condition is certainly a possibility; however, this becomes questionable if there is no hope of achieving the quality or meaning of what has been lost. This reservation will always apply for works of art, as well as for the decorative work of specialist craftsmen. Such considerations have, for instance, obviously informed Anderhalten Architects' conversion of the plenar hall in the Academy of Sciences in Berlin.

The Redoutensaal in the Hofburg Palace in Vienna was re-erected in its original volume after extensive fire damage but using modern fittings, to serve as an attractive events' hall of the congress centre (Manfred Wehdorn, 1997).

Of all the different approaches to adaptation, the strategy of CONVERSION has been most widely adopted among architects in the past. Throughout the ages, architects have employed a whole palette of architectural options ranging from slight to radical reorganisations of the floor plan, modifications to the structural system, the reconfiguration of circulation and access, and the adaptation of architectural forms according to prevailing taste. In most cases the conversion maintains the basic structure and floor levels of the existing building, occasionally removing sections of the floor to improve the long-term usability of the spaces in the building. Conversion concentrates primarily on the redesign of the existing spaces and the adaptation of the building to a new use.

It can be particularly enriching when conversion measures reveal parts or even entire sections of past interiors in all their splendour. Major European cities such as Basel, Zürich, Regensburg or Lübeck attribute part of their regained attraction to the efforts invested in investigating and revealing their specific historic treasures, also with regard to individual and attractive interiors. Here, modern materials and furnishings underline the role of interior design.

The war-damaged hall of the Academy of Sciences in Berlin was reconstructed in a simplified form (Claus Anderhalten, 2003).

A special case of conversion works, particularly relevant and popular in inner-city areas, is the ROOF CONVERSION. The relationship of new openings or dormers on the roof to the overall appearance of the building must be considered carefully. The overwhelming desire to maximise the use of available space has clouded our appreciation of its effect on the roofscapes of towns and cities, as well as our awareness of the problems associated with using roof spaces, such as the provision of an escape route in the event of fire and appropriate insulation. The insulation of the roof covering is seldom sufficient to ensure a comfortable interior during periods of prolonged high temperatures. Additional ventilation measures will need to be planned to dissipate the warmth that collects beneath the roof without the need for environmentally unsound air conditioning. Care should also be taken to correctly detail vapour-permeable membranes to ensure sufficient vapour diffusion.

The recovered medieval timber-planked room is a well-accepted and dignified space for the head of the local authority in the newly converted town hall in Wels, Austria.

The EXTENSION is a further common strategy for continuing to use a building and has been employed for thousands of years. When an existing building no longer provides sufficient space, it is extended, either in the form of new buildings or upwards as a new storey, and in some cases even downwards underground. In recent decades, architectural discourse has explored the relationship of new extensions to the origi-

Staircase in the keep.

Exhibition room.

A museum in a Tyrolean landmark

Tyrolean Museum of History, 2003
Tyrol Castle, Italy
Client: Independent province of Bolzano
Architect: Scherer & Angonese / Hellweger

Tirol Castle is one of the oldest and most important castles in the Alps. The majority of the existing building dates back to the 12th century. Based upon comprehensive building research and archaeological investigation, the complex was converted to a municipal museum between 2000 and 2003. The historic building fabric from the different ages is maintained as it was. It serves as an exhibit in itself, the phases of the structure documenting the complex history of the region. The often exposed historic walls are contrasted with modern insertions, also made of exposed materials. A carefully designed lighting concept highlights the contrast between the irregular existing fabric and the smooth new insertions.

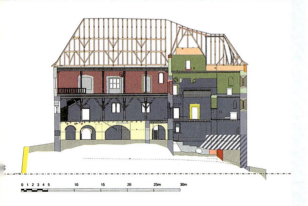

Section with archaeological analysis.

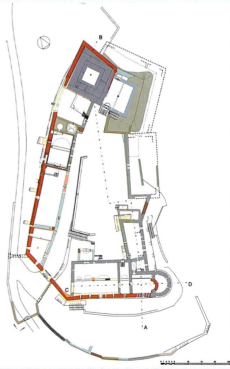

Floor plan showing the building phases of the overall complex.

nal context in form and design. In tight inner-city plots where space is limited, the architect should first examine the remaining space between the building and the neighbour. In many cases this is the most promising option of mobilising space. When building alongside an existing building, a key question is how both parts connect with one another. This is not only a question of form, but also a technical and organisational problem. It is important to know the exact heights of the existing floor levels, including any deformations, as well as to clarify the nature of the construction against which one will be building.

The notion that an existing building can remain unchanged through the addition of a new extension is rarely true in reality. Even when no building works are undertaken in the old building, new access, openings and connections must be created to connect the two, and this often leads to a change in the way the existing building is accessed and used.

The industrial character of the building on the outskirts of Milan, Italy, takes the roof as its cue and creates a complex living space (Francesca Donati, 2001).

If insufficient floor area is available for an extension, the ADDITION OF A NEW STOREY can serve the same basic purpose. Of particular importance when planning an additional storey is the question of access and the provision of an escape route in the event of fire. It is important to clarify this question using the available documentation before suggesting this option to the client. Local firemen must be able to reach the building from the outside (max. ladder height), and in addition, the extra storey may also have fire resistance implications for the existing staircase. Whilst it generally makes sense to organise the new storey according to the pattern of load-bearing walls, numerous projects have shown that attractive alternative solutions are also possible. The addition of a new storey necessarily involves sacrificing the roof construction, and this must be considered carefully, in particular when roof constructions are historically important, which may be the case for constructions built before the early 20th century. It is also important to bear in mind that the

Roof conversion after completion.

Roof conversion after completion.

Model.

New floor plans.

Adaptations to a residential area

Conversion of single family houses, 2004
Utrecht, Netherlands
Client: private
Architect: ZECC Architects

The terraced houses in a residential area on the edge of Utrecht date back to 1900, no longer fulfil current technical standards and are too small for most families. The uniformity of the architecture is slightly oppressive. Roof dormers were added to individual buildings in the row, giving it a new urban texture and making the individual houses more unique. Although the basic strategy is identical, each dormer has a different appearance, with different materials and slightly varying forms according to the wishes of the inhabitants. The additions give the row a more articulated urban form.

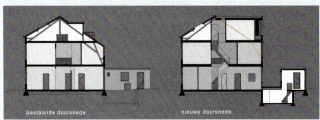

Cross section of a house before and after conversion.

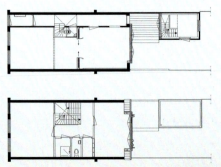

Modernisation of a bank

Conversion of a historic office building, 2002
Zurich, Switzerland
Client: Credit Suisse
Architect: Atelier 5

The neo-classical Schweizerische Kreditanstalt, constructed in 1877 and altered again in 1899, needed fundamental modernisation whilst respecting the different building phases. Consequently, the architects' concept draws on the history of the structure. Numerous later additions that had disfigured the building were removed and emphasis was given to highlighting the elaborate material treatment of the historic rooms. Additional offices were created in the interior courtyard of the building. In places it was also necessary to reorganise the access to the offices. New metal and glass partition walls were inserted into the access areas to fulfil modern requirements and fire safety regulations. A consistent colour concept provides clarity and orientation within the building.

The central customer service hall is now used for access and circulation.

Circulation areas are partitioned off with additional glass walls.

The historic façade has remained largely unchanged.

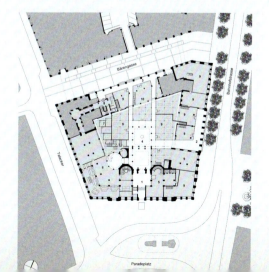

Additional offices were created in the internal courtyard.

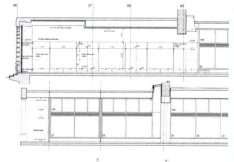

Detail drawing.

The new circulation in an extensive complex of old buildings used by the University in Toledo, Spain, makes use of the old courtyard to reorganise the entire complex (AUIA, 1993).

wall plate and joists of the roof level are often not as strong as those for the lower floors.

The UNDERPINNING of a building in order to insert additional storeys below ground, although now increasingly common in urban areas, is a strategy with only limited implications for architectural design.

Where an extension is not possible, for whatever reasons, the COMBINATION of several buildings for a single common purpose is a further means of overcoming functional limitations by developing existing buildings. The disadvantages are however often considerable, especially when neighbouring buildings were built at different times and have uneven floor levels and heights. Openings made from one building to the next will almost always result in the need for special solutions to overcome differences in height. Often the skilful placement of a new common staircase with stepped landings at the floor heights of each building can overcome this problem, however, it can become particularly complex where disabled access is necessary. The unification of several individual buildings

Cubic roof additions to a house in Graz, Austria, transform an otherwise unremarkable building (INNOCAD, 2001).

The Architects' Building in Moscow: classical core with an overly modern addition (Asadov, 2006).

into one large building is almost always a problem as each building has its own load-bearing structure. It makes little sense to transform a series of individual buildings at great cost and to rob each of its identity in order to create a building that would be simpler and more cost-effective to erect elsewhere using other means.

An exception to this rule is when existing buildings are left more or less as they are and united under a common roof. The lightweight structures from the 1970s are a model for this kind of approach. The artificiality of this approach, which has been borrowed from landscape design, is readily apparent, but, as well-known projects by famous architects continue to demonstrate, it can still be very appealing.

Replacement

From time to time, an architect may come across a building, or part of a building, that has reached the end of its useful life, where no amount of maintenance will improve its condition, and modernisation amounts to rebuilding entire sections of the building. In such cases there is usually no sensible alternative but to demolish the building, taking care to dispose of its materials ecologically. Whether one decides to save a particular element, either for nostalgic reasons, or to incorporate it into a new replacement building, is a matter of personal preference. At what point the decision to demolish and RENEW the building should be made is dependent upon each situation. Although a demolition may appear simpler than complex repairs, the decision to renew should not be made lightly, both for reasons of sustainability and of cultural identity. Where cities are shrinking and vacant buildings are demolished, the lack of adequate follow-up uses has led to dramatic consequences: the replacement of buildings with car parks rapidly leads to an impoverished quality of life.

The remnant as generator for the design of a new building: historical analysis and remnants found in excavations determine the face of the new townhouse on Friedrichswerder, Berlin (Marc Jordi, 2006).

The most common reason for demolishing or gutting a part of the building is not, however, defects in the existing construction, but the desire to achieve a radically different building structure. In many cases all that actually remains is the historic façade as a symbol of the original building and a concession to the townscape. This approach can be regarded as an extreme version of fragmentation. The justification is usually the assumption, rarely correct, that it is easier to build a new building on the foundations of the old building than to work within the constraints of the old building.

This approach cannot produce good architecture. The detachment of the façade from its original context and structural basis and its independence from the new replacement building is a poor compromise that results in an unhappy splicing of new and old, and is an approach that is better resisted.

If one were to classify a building according to the amount of original building substance remaining, then the remodelling of the Reichstag in Berlin by Sir Norman Foster or the Castelgrande in Bellinzona by Aurelio Galfetti would count as new buildings. The Reichstag was completely gutted. In the interiors, the only remaining traces of a hundred years of history are the graffiti scratched into the walls by Russian soldiers in 1945. No interiors of the old Reichstag from 1894 are still in place, likewise no trace of the Reichstag fire in 1933, or of damage sustained during the Second World War or of Paul Baumgarten's sparse reconstruction after the war. Similarly, the Castelgrande in Bellinzona bore numerous traces of history and different uses in its lifetime. The conversion has removed all of these including all fittings in favour of a completely new design. The results of both projects are magnificent, though their relation to their history is almost entirely one of image; almost all of the original building substance has been lost.

The former elevation as decorative element of the modern new building on the corner of Rossmarkt, Frankfurt am Main, Germany (Jean Nouvel).

What an architect chooses to build on a cleared plot is not the subject of this book. However, one special case continues to fascinate the public to the present day: the RECONSTRUCTION of important historic buildings that have previously been lost. Although some commentators think otherwise, a new building that is built in the form of a historic building, regardless of how well-researched and executed it may be, remains a new building and as such a contemporary architectural statement.

The aim of a reconstruction project is often associated with the desire to recover a valuable piece of architecture. After traumatic periods of loss in particular, the need to recover at least some of what was lost through reconstruction was great, as it were reversing the loss, and classifying a historically irreversible fact an "error" or "wrongdoing" of history. A prominent example is the rebuilding of the old city of Warsaw right after the Second World War. A more recent example is the reconstruction of the Frauenkirche in Dresden, completed in 2005. Both symbolise a new beginning for the inhabitants of these cities. In Warsaw the buildings were rebuilt on their original floor plans using the remaining rubble, but in the contemporary architectural form of the 1950s. As such they only give an impression of what was lost. In Dresden, however, the impression is that we can make it possible to literally resurrect the original.

Any reasonable person will agree that it is impossible to regain something that has been destroyed. If hypothetically, a lost painting by Rembrandt were to be repainted from photographs made of the original, neither experts nor the general public would view it as an actual Rembrandt. It could never replace the original and the reproduction is known to be simply a rendition of the original. The same principle applies to architecture.

The new Frauenkirche in Dresden is not the product of Georg Baer and his master craftsmen, but of their 21st century counterparts. This "major work of the Baroque age" has not been recovered, but has been rendered in the form of a reconstruction.

In addition to this, most architectural reconstructions are a poor rendition of the past, often no more than a rather generalised image of a point in history. Few people are prepared to invest the high cost of appropriate planning and constructional realisation, which in most cases would far exceed the actual value of the building. Manufacturing and production conditions change so rapidly that it becomes virtually impossible to repeat building processes from even the comparatively recent past. The results of reconstructions are therefore almost always new buildings with a contemporary layout behind façades which more or less successfully imitate history.

The uneasy relationship many architects have to such hybridised compromise-reconstructions is understandable, as they no longer fulfil the long-standing canons of good architecture such as harmony of form and content, and unity of construction and materials.

The attempt to reconstruct a building whose material substance has been lost may on the one hand be viewed as paying respect to the past and its achievements, but on the other hand it also reveals a deep-seated fear in our society as well as among architects of what the future will bring, together with a latent mistrust in the capabilities of today's architects.

ARCHITECTONIC EXPRESSION

However good a design concept or strategy, the final result will also be determined by the formal and aesthetic qualities of the overall design. Conservationists and supporters of sustainability may argue about the degree of original building fabric that has been retained in a project – whether we actually like the end result is a matter of each and every person's individual taste. Building legislation aims to achieve a balance between the owner and the architect's right to freedom of taste on the one hand, and the right of the public at large to a qualitative environment on the other. Local design guides set out guidelines that ensure that developments are compatible with the local environment. Given these constraints, relevant design questions include how the new relates to the old, whether interventions are visible or not, and, often of the most interest to the public, whether the design is bold and striking or reserved and restrained. The possibilities range from the extremes of integrative conformity to defiant contrast.

Historic front, glazed rear: the new Kommandantur (commandant's headquarters) on the boulevard Unter den Linden in Berlin (Thomas van den Valentyn, 2003).

Every design made in the context of existing structures will need to address the issue of how new additions connect with or differentiate themselves from what already exists. This fundamental question has characterised discourse on design in historic contexts in all periods, and has brought forward a variety of often emphatic opinions. This is where hierarchies are determined: whether the new design subordinates itself to the old building, or whether it stands out through conspicuous design or choice of materials.

Correspondence

The continuation of existing forms and architectural means is a simple approach to harmonising the new with the old. Where the same or similar constructions, materials, colours and forms are used for new buildings and where extensions correspond to the basic volume, eaves, cornice lines, and roof form of the original, the result will be harmonious – but also probably a little lacklustre.

The slight differences between the original and the new building, however, provide room for expression. In recent years in particular, many architectural concepts exhibit a desire to continue the basic structure, idea and often also proportions of an existing building, but at the same time to create something new and independent by sensitively modifying these basic principles. The new design distinguishes itself from the existing building through subtle differentiation rather than direct contrast. Wood remains wood, but a different kind of wood is chosen. Through the careful selection of materials and artistic means, the new element resonates with the old. By engaging with the craftsmanship of the original, a dialogue between new and old can result: a whisper of difference that describes the natural succession of time and the process of continual renewal. Drawing on tradition, such as the use of materials or regional styles and typologies, need not necessarily be folksy; it can provide a grammar from which a new architectonic expression can result. The continuation of tradition has the added advantage of harmoniously connecting with the original and avoiding structural or technical ruptures. Building upon tradition also strengthens regional identity and can even enliven entire sectors of the local economy, as the regions of Vorarlberg and Graubünden in the Alps or the Norwegian architecture school have demonstrated so successfully in the 1980s and 1990s. This form of correspondence adopts only selected aspects from tradition, in the process transforming them into a new expression that builds upon but distances itself from the past.

Harmonisation is, however, not without risks. The belief that quality is automatically assured when new elements correspond exactly with the original often ends in dissatisfactory results. Where the new corresponds entirely with the old, it communicates a false impression of history and a lack of design initiative. On the other hand, the arbitrary incorporation of elements from the past will appear just as devoid of meaning. When drawing a correspondence between new and old, the skill is to weigh-up the typological strengths of the old and to interpret these imaginatively using modern means.

An extension in the tradition of workmanship

Swimming pool extension to a manor house
Spexhall Manor, Great Britain
Client: private
Architect: Purcell Miller Tritton

The manor house dates back to the 17th century and was fundamentally remodelled in 1908. Following a change of ownership, it was decided to upgrade the building to meet modern standards and provide contemporary comforts. This included the creation of extensive recreational facilities and a swimming pool. The decision to adapt and extend the existing building in the same form as the original led to a doubling of the original volume and duplication of the material and workmanship of the original building. A casual visitor will not notice immediately that significant parts of the complex are new. This is largely due to the exacting workmanship and careful detailing of the new additions, which continue the principle of the original.

Elevation drawings of the old manor house with the extension.

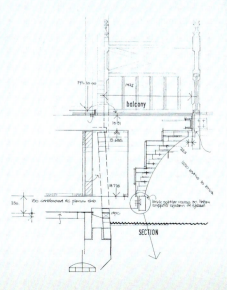

Exterior view of the swimming pool with the old house in the background.

The historic manor house.

Interior of the new building with seating area and swimming pool.

Working drawing.

The "Weltsaal" after conversion works.

The post scanning centre – a new addition in the inner courtyard.

Floor plan of overall complex.

The foyer.

Built continuity

German Federal Foreign Office in the former Reichsbank, 1940/1999
Berlin, Germany
Client: Federal Republic of Germany
Architects: Hans Kollhoff/Helga Timmermann

The former Reichsbank building was constructed from 1933 to 1940 by Heinrich Wolff and furnished luxuriously but not lavishly. It survived the Second World War largely unscathed and after refitting continued to be used by the GDR authorities. After the reunification of Germany in 1989, the demolishing of the building for ideological reasons was briefly considered before it was decided to convert it for use as the Federal Foreign Office. The design respects the basic arrangement of the building, clears it of most of the additions made in GDR times, and continues the tradition of the original building, using high-quality but conservative fittings and finishes but without imitating it in the slightest. The design aims to be a built continuation of the existing building but with a contemporary spirit.

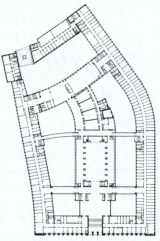

The entrance hall in the Nazi era, 1945.

The entrance hall in GDR, 1989.

The entrance hall in the Federal Republic of Germany, 2000.

Unification

A building that has grown with time, undergoing a series of alterations in the process, is almost always complex and irregular. Some architects and clients value precisely this characteristic and have made it the starting point for their design. Whilst this can be instructive, the demonstrative presentation of historical fragments, regardless of how important they may be, has becomes so widespread in recent years that it has provoked a counter approach in which importance of historical traces is played down in favour of the formal presentation of the building as a unified whole. In the 1970s, there was a similar reaction to the colourful experiments of the 1950s, and many buildings were replastered and painted in sober colours resulting in a more cubist and uniform appearance. Whenever the spirit of the age admires the clarity of large forms and clear gestures, many existing buildings are FORMALLY UNIFIED using colour or materials. Walls with complex structures or varying materiality can be made to appear more uniform by applying a paint or stain in the same colour to all surfaces. The lining of all walls with a new layer serves the same purpose. Here, the old surface is conserved unchanged behind the new lining without the need for any extra investment. The new lining or colour treatment lays down its own set of formal parameters. This solution has many advantages over and above visual unification: it conserves the existing fabric and is largely independent of the construction. Whether the new layer is a simple lining made of plasterboard or a lavishly executed work of art is a matter of the architect's design intention, and applies equally indoors as well as for the redesign of elevations. The strategy of formal unification is most appropriate where the historic value of a building is comparatively insignificant and the course of history has resulted in a confused agglomeration of different forms. In such cases, the use of varied design treatments in response to the variety of forms only serves to exacerbate their irregularity.

The Sainsbury Wing of the National Gallery in London continues the architecture of the original, interpreting it anew (Robert Venturi, 1991).

141

The face of the Traumbaum-Kindergarten in Berlin is completely transformed by the imaginative insertion (Baupiloten, 2003).

The REMODELLING OF FAÇADES of historic buildings has been a favourite preoccupation of architects through the ages. The face of a house was and still is changed even when only slight alterations are made to the building itself. In the past the primary motive for such alterations was to lend a degree of order and structure to irregularly placed windows. Today, in addition to improving the energy efficiency of the building's skin, elevation remodelling aims to give the building a clear identity and a contemporary appearance. Once again, the arrangement of the windows, whether symmetrical or freely arranged, offers the greatest potential for design.

Where the unification of different buildings cannot be achieved by means of remodelling the elevations, two or more buildings can be integrated by means of a new UNIFYING STRUCTURE, be it a new elevation or a common roof structure. The old structures disappear behind a new element. In principle the existing buildings can continue to be used as they are. However, the new element often changes the constellation of the existing buildings, and new spaces, in particular for circulation, can improve the way in which they are used.

In addition to the formal unification of a building complex, the RECONSTRUCTION OF A HISTORIC CONDITION from the building's history is without doubt also a form of unification. The reconstruction of a previous state – often the initial, original condition of the building, in as far as this is known – is particularly popular because it gives the building a specific identity which many people can relate to. It is easy to define the aims of such projects, they lead to clearly visible results and are generally well-received by the public. Some reconstructions are even undertaken with the support of the conservation authorities. The aim is usually the historicised restoration of "impaired" urban ensembles. For individual buildings, the motive is the reproduction of a past situation or the smoothing over of design inconsistencies.

All such decisions result in the eradication of a variety of subsequent historic traces, often tragic or disturbing ones, and create an artificial condition, in which it appears that time has stood still without further development. Whether this is for an individual building or an urban ensemble, what is required is the experience and services of conservators and restoration contractors rather than the services of a creative architect. Here the conflict between history as an individual point in time, and the single-minded desire to reconstruct this moment on the one hand, and history as a succession of developments and sequence of events on the other hand, becomes clear. Architecture, through its often remarkable longevity and versatility, is able to testify to both. It can convey history both in terms of image as well as building substance. In this respect, the reconstruction preserves a moment in time, a unified and aesthetic image of its time, but often in conflict with the reality of a changing world.

The Haus der Presse by Wolfgang Hänsch (1961) in Dresden, Germany: once an Avant-garde building from GDR times, now with a remodelled façade of screen-printed glass panels (Martin Seelinger, 2003).

Fragmentation

Ever since Carlo Scarpa's masterly MISE-EN-SCÈNE of history in his remodelling of the Castelvecchio Museum in Verona from 1964 elevated the potential of historical finds to its central theme, the dissection and fragmentation of a building into individual elements has become one of the most important means of incorporating history into a design. The use of historical analysis as a generator for the architectonic design can invest a design concept with meaning. It leads to highly individual solutions and forms a complex system of references. For many designs adopting this approach, the physical dissection of the existing building is a popular starting point. Sometimes it is sufficient to simply remove the most recent layer of wallpaper and paint to open a window onto the past. It is not uncommon, once the wood-chip wallpaper has been removed, to find the remains of previous wall decorations: stencil and roller patterns, painted timber panelling or wall panels. In many cases, these will have been damaged or even destroyed by the later insertion of technical installations. Nevertheless, these traces of the past seem to exert considerable fascination, and the popularity of uncovering such traces as a means of lending interest to shops, restaurants and bars is positively uncanny. In most cases, these traces serve as little more than an eye-catcher. The message they convey is limited, primarily because no indication of the meaning of the fragment is provided – and arguably is of little interest to the owner.

When the removal of wallpaper reveals little of interest, the plasterwork is often also removed. The brick masonry, concrete or stonework beneath is revealed, often exhibiting traces of alterations and changes. What one reads into such alterations is another question. Although the problem of loose grit from the mortar joints of exposed brickwork walls is widespread and difficult to control, the display of exposed constructions, although never originally intended to be seen that way, remains as popular as ever. The work of Scarpa, Carmassi or Canali, as well as of numerous other architects since the 1990s, is unthinkable without such revelatory design methods.

Café Silberstein in Berlin. The 1920s wall mural has been revealed and left unchanged. The contrast between new and old lends the room a special character.

Massimo Carmassi is in this respect a master at developing a stimulating juxtaposition of broken fragments, delicate artistic surfaces and skilfully designed new elements out of a seemingly incoherent collection of remaining fragments. The central aim of such fragmentary approaches is not to explain historical interrelationships but for the visitor or inhabitant to marvel at the surprises the building has to offer and the historical distance between the finish of "today" and the broken fragments of "the past". This historical distance can only be perceived if both "today" and "the past" are present wherever one looks. This implies that such illustrative solutions are not possible without a considerable flurry of visual detail.

This illustrative effect becomes even clearer, the stronger the difference between new and old is. The complexity of a historic building, its materiality, surfaces and colours already provides for much interest on its own. When a design adds new elements – a new building volume or a building element – this often is clearly differentiated from the existing building. If the old plaster is rough, the new plaster is often smooth; if the old staircase is made of wood, the new is often made of steel. Once the new element has been completed and is ready for use, the old element appears worn, old and no longer sufficient alongside it. This approach – consciously or subconsciously – results effectively in a depreciation of the old building substance in comparison to the new. The once fully functional old building is reduced to a picturesque showpiece. The original intention to bring out the qualities and value of the building has actually resulted in the opposite. The fascination with the portrayal of new and old is less interested in the value of the old building as an integral whole, and is more about the fading memory of it. Even the most masterful practitioners of this approach did not act in the interests of conservation when designing their fragmentation strategies. On the contrary, the arbitrary and unrelenting interventions made to otherwise intact buildings by Scarpa in Castelvecchio and Schattner in the Museum of the Diocese in Eichstätt, are enough to make any conservator's hair stand

The drama of new and old in a former farmhouse in Lans, Austria, transformed by precisely placed interventions (Martin Scharfetter, 2004).

on end. Little more than the external walls remain of the castle in Verona, and the defect-free and fully functional timber construction of the former warehouse in Eichstätt as Schattner found it, could no doubt have served as a museum without modification – the elaborate cable-truss supporting the cut-off posts is an artistic decision rather than one dictated by function.

Historical analysis is also the basis for a DIDACTIC DESIGN approach, which attempts to communicate the value of the historic building substance, its historical references and meaning by systematically uncovering pieces of its history and making these generators for the design concept. The basic intention to make the individual characteristics of the building legible and so lend the building a historic and social dimension is particularly enticing: many owners buy old houses for exactly this reason. The investment is often also cost-effective. Interesting finds made in the building also serve quite simply as decoration, obviating the need for "art installations" and are typically well-received by the general public. Whether left visible as they are or specially presented at certain times, they offer a window to the past, and serve as attractions for tourists and even more so for the inhabitants and users; a restored historic find serves both as a nostalgic reminder of an often subconsciously idolised notion of the past as well as a novel decorative element. And what has proved so successful for presenting relics of the building fabric can likewise be applied to rendered elevations.

As far back as the 1960s Polish restorers and conservators recognised the potential of historic finds as a central theme for the design of building elevations, in the process ennobling and stimulating interest in the history of buildings. Although today such demonstrative approaches are viewed with a degree of scepticism, there can be no doubt that the integration of historic finds in building elevations, when presented discreetly and in moderation, is seen favourably by the general public.

A further approach to the art of fragmentation is one of deliberate ALIENATION or DEFAMILIARISATION. The original building is maintained in its material substance but either its surfaces or its tectonics are so radically transformed, that the message the building conveys is changed, resulting in an entirely new character. Going beyond the strategy of contrasting new and old, deliberate alteration of the existing configuration creates a formal differentiation between different historic periods and what is new, in this way expressing change. Through its very contradictory nature, this form of fragmentation makes reference to a society that has lost its clear idea of the world, using means similar to those of deconstructivism to replace it with a reflection of the splintered nature and arbitrariness of the world. Other techniques, including the ironic "falsification" of finds such as in Karljosef Schattner's "revelations" in his Ulmer Hof project, adopt a similar approach. They illustrate the flexibility of defamiliarisation strategies and their ability to portray very different prevailing moods.

Some designers revel in the playful folding of old and new layers into a complex representation of reality expressed through the architecture. One effective game of deception is the reversal of inside and outside; indeed, many extensions result in outside becoming inside as a matter of course, a natural consequence of the growth of a building. In the Architecture Museum in Frankfurt by Oswald Mathias Ungers, this strategy is used to stimulate a profound consideration on architecture itself.

Hidden beneath the plaster of a building in Spandau, Berlin, Germany, are numerous historic finds from the late medieval period.

The history of the "Koberg 2" building in Lübeck, Germany, disappears behind a flap. Curious visitors can discover for themselves.

Deliberate alienation: the modern stair winds upwards over the Roman mosaic in the Franciscan monastery in Porec, Croatia. The pierced rubble wall is painted black.

The old roof panels of St. Valentin am Forst, Austria, parish church are re-laid in an artistic form on the new extension and document the relationship of new and old (Reinhard Gieselmann, 1992).

The council chamber in Perchtoldsdorf, Austria: the upper part of the room retains its historic decoration, the lower part receives modern fixtures and furnishings (Hans Hollein, 1976).

Theatrical contrasts

Town hall conversion and extension, 1999
Utrecht, Netherlands
Client: City of Utrecht
Architect: Enric Miralles

Utrecht town hall originates from medieval times and has a long history of complex alterations. The extension of the administrative facilities into neighbouring buildings necessitated a reassessment of the distribution of functions. A detailed analysis of the existing building fabric provided the basis for the new design. A new council chamber was created in the upper storey of the old building and the circulation reorganised completely.

The design concept contrasts the new with the old, providing carefully orchestrated surprises throughout the building. The almost complete demolition and fragmentary rebuilding of the north wing, and the design of the foyer and the meeting rooms all follow this principle. Material, colour, artistic expression and interior design are used in a variety of ways to intentionally contrast with the existing building.

General view after the conversion.

The foyer with pictures arranged in an apparently random fashion across the walls.

In the meeting room, remnants of historic fixtures are set against seemingly chaotic modern elements.

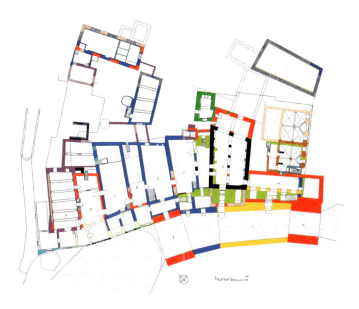

The building phase plan – the basis for the conversion proposal.

The lecture hall as a new element between the old walls.

General view of the building from 1940.

Lecture room in a monumental building

Conversion of the arcades of the Nuevos Ministerios, 1940/2004
Madrid, Spain
Client: Ministerio de la Vivienda
Architect: Jesús Aparicio Guisado and Héctor Fernández-Elorza

A section of the arcades of a government ministry building, erected in the monumental style of the Franco era, was to be converted for use as a multi-purpose lecture room. The project attempts to respect the existing building and to introduce an independent and modern solution into the controversial architecture of the original. The new insertion is separated from the existing structure and differentiates itself from the irregular surfaces of the original through their smooth facing and deliberately chosen delineation between new and old. The space between the insertion and the existing structure serves as an installation duct and climate buffer. In this way technical requirements complement the design solution.

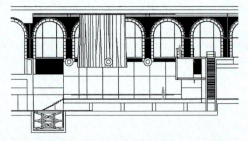

The design of the new entrance frees itself from the existing monumental architecture.

The smooth new insertion contrasts with the existing building.

Longitudinal schematic section showing scissor-lift stage and projection room.

Junction and delineation

The way in which the new and the old are brought together determines whether the existing building plays a leading or a supporting role. At the point where they join one can read the value ascribed by the architect to the existing building, and his or her position with regard to the historical continuity of architecture in general. This is where the attempt at integration or the balance of the relationship is measured, and where the success of references or allusions is made or broken. Although the junction is undoubtedly a critical point, one should be aware that the overall design will be more convincing when the underlying principle behind the junction of new and old is also apparent in the treatment of both parts of the project. Shadow lines and changes of material are devices not limited to either the new or the old building.

The principle of delineation applies at both large and small scales, whether in the overall composition of the building volumes, for instance through the introduction of a glazed section often serving no other purpose than the transition between buildings, or in the junction between two different materials using a shadow line. From a construction point of view, a movement joint is essential as new building constructions have different internal movement dynamics to old, settled building structures. However, it does make a fundamental difference whether the meeting of different ages is consciously expressed or allowed to happen silently.

In almost all designs made in the context of existing buildings, the JOINT is the primary visual delineator of the bipolarity of new and old, and a separation of the past and the present. In its function as separator and bridge, the design of the joint must be carefully considered and expressed accordingly. The same basic design treatments used for the coexistence of old and new building substance also apply for the composition of additions and extensions to old buildings. Contrast and composition are similarly valid concepts beyond the expression of material traces of history. If the old building is varied and highly decorative, the new building often is deliberately plain and unadorned; where the old building is large enough, the new addition often nestles in behind it, or alternatively deliberately towers over it; if the old building has a pitched roof, the new addition is often given a flat roof; where the old building is half-timbered, the new building is often rendered in stone or as facing concrete, and so on.

A common approach to delineating two parts of a building from different periods is to insert a clearly perceptible glazed element between them. In

The extensive new additions to the Teyler Museum in Haarlem connect only occasionally with the old buildings via narrow glass corridors (Hubert-Jan Henket, 1994).

contrast to the past, where the technical possibilities of glass were not available and great effort was invested in interlocking the bonding of masonry, today the transition between two buildings has been reduced to a glazed slot, often frameless. The transparent slot delineates the historic process of addition and growth; from a technical point of view, it also serves to mediate between the thermal movement of both structures. Where an internal separation between new and old is not necessary, many designers have found it sufficient to express the delineation of new and old as a simple recess or gap.

The apparent immateriality of glass makes it an ideal building material for delineation as it is neutral, avoiding the need to express a particular design approach. However, other devices for junction and separation are also possible, for instance a change of material or a deliberate change of surface treatment. The hand-applied render or plaster of an old building may be uneven and irregular. A smooth surface such as a fine-grade facing concrete, painted metal or planed wood creates sufficient contrast. Even a change from rough plaster to smooth plaster is sufficient to indicate where two parts of a building meet.

In conservation practice, it is common to differentiate repairs from the original through a change of colour in the mortar used. Italian renovation practice employs a technique called *sotto livello* in which the new plaster is applied less thickly so that it remains behind the level of the original plaster. A change in level is a further device used to delineate different areas in architectural design. Straightforward continuation of the original surfaces and alignment only rarely produces satisfactory results. Clearly perceptible projections or recesses, overhangs or the set back arrangement of new building volumes are usually more successful approaches.

The new circulation for the parish centre at Klingenmünster, Germany, is independent of the historic building and resolves the transition using a glass strip (Auer/Cramer/Frotscher, 1995).

The SHADOW LINE is a traditional means of architectonic expression and it is no surprise that it plays an important role in the junction and delineation of different parts of buildings. Few other solutions embody the aspects of separation and transition so naturally.

The use of the expressed join as an architectonic device is questionable when its artistic elaboration exceeds the event it marks, for example where a deep recess separates a small addition to a family house or where a glass slot provides the transition to an otherwise unimportant lean-to. Seen from the future, such elaborately demonstrative joints may appear all the more excessive once the new element has also aged and undergoes further transformations – from a future standpoint the difference in age will be less obvious than from the present.

A joint is also necessary where one building PENETRATES another, at the point where the old and the new intersect. In this case the joint serves a purpose that is primarily structural rather than of architectonic expression. The concept of penetration already embodies a degree of appropriation of the other, and such designs will usually be demonstrative enough without the need for further elaboration of the junction. When the device of penetration involves breaking open the building fabric, it can be attributed to the

General view of the glass-covered court.

Deliberate transitions

British Museum, Queen Elizabeth II Great Court, 2003
London, Great Britain
Client: The British Museum
Architect: Sir Norman Foster

The integration of the courtyard into the museum circulation, including a new visitors' level, several flights of stairs and a glazed roof, introduces many new elements into the old structure. The junction between old and new is not left to chance but is the product of a consistent design strategy: separation and transition is a conscious act, whether as a glass bridge between the old structure and the central rotunda, a glass strip between the new floor level and the original façade or a metal-lined recess between existing building and new stair. The same principle is applied in both the old and the new building. Similarly, a discreet but perceptible recess separates the glazed roof from the walls of the old structure.

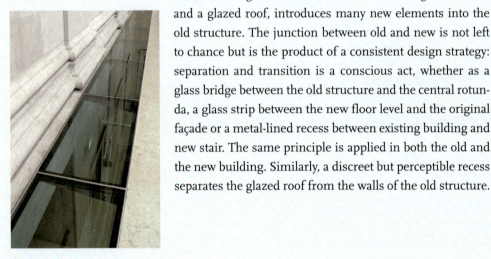

The visitors' level is separated from the façade of the old building by a glass strip.

A narrow joint delineates the boundary between the new floor and the old façade.

The glass bridge connects the central rotunda with the museum galleries.

approach of fragmentation. Where it is used to present an individual artefact or fragment, it may also serve to abstract this fragment from its original context. The portrayal of this formal device will inevitably involve a contrast of material and form, presenting an image to the viewer that describes the process of intrusion.

This device can be used to deliberate effect to differentiate the present from the past. The almost brutal piercing and BREAKING OPEN of a monolithic construction from the Nazi period and its penetration with a new element provides enough conceptual distance to allow the politically correct utilisation of the building. The drawn-out process of dismantling the Palast der Republik in Berlin, the former political and cultural headquarters of the GDR, can be seen in a similar context. Here the artistic intention is to portray the process of dismantling as a contrasting image to that of the sudden demolition of the Palace that previously stood in its place. If architectural mise-en-scène has its origins in theatre, then the architectonic event is a natural progression of this. With it the process of formal fragmentation acquires a temporal dimension not usually associated with architecture.

The new Sackler Galleries of the Royal Academy of Arts in London has a glass strip in the floor at the point where it meets the façade of the old building, allowing one to still comprehend the old elevation (Norman Foster, 1991).

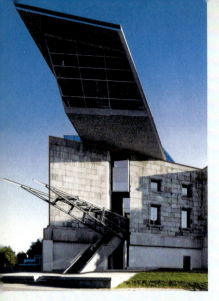

View of the entrance situation.

Axonometric drawing of the entire complex with the new building.

A thorn in the side of Nazi architecture

Documentation centre of the former Nazi party rally grounds, 2001
Nuremberg, Germany
Client: Town council of Nuremberg
Architect: Günther Domenig

The congress building on the former Nazi party rally grounds in Nuremberg remained a ruin for decades after the end of the Second World War. The documentation centre, created at the end of the 1990s, takes the contradictory nature of the ideologically stigmatised site as its theme and breaks it open with a precisely formed and bizarre construction that pierces the building diagonally. The artificiality of the new building contrasts strongly with the former Nazi building. The fracturing of the building is desirable and demonstrative.

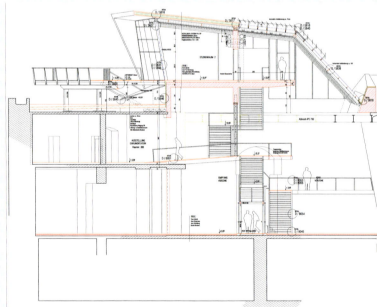

Interior view showing the penetration of the old with the new.

Cross section of the new building.

Further reading

A comprehensive guide to architectural design in the context of existing buildings has not existed up to now. BROOKER/STONE have presented a volume with particular emphasis on the aesthetics and LINHARDT has demonstrated some aspects for the conversion of houses. The many available case study volumes available testify to the general relevance of this topic (HERBERS, LERCH, POWELL, SCHITTICH, SCHLEIFER, SIMON). Some of these include extensive introductory essays on background issues (MASTROPIETRO, SPITAL-FRENKING, THIÉBAUT, WALZ). The WÜSTENROT STIFTUNG organised two design competitions in 1999 and 2006 and the results are systematically documented together with essays in printed form.

As far back as 1932, GUTSCHOW/ZIPPEL undertook a fundamental examination of conversion, though it had little effect. MEYER-BOHE examines many aspects associated with extensions. Deliberations of HOESLI and the SMITHSONS have been published in rather marginal contexts.

The surface of the repairs to the masonry is set back slightly from the level of the original masonry (sotto livello), indicating the difference between the original and the repairs and signifying the passage of time.

157

DETAIL PLANNING

*The image of a preserved memory, to be protected, is for me the reference point.**

Andrea Bruno

In the design of a new building, an appealing concept may distract attention from weaknesses in the detailed execution. However, for projects involving historic or existing buildings, it is primarily the quality of the design of details and individual solutions that will determine the character of the end result. Countless architects, from Karl Friedrich Schinkel to Carlo Scarpa, from Michelangelo to Sir Norman Foster, have demonstrated this impressively in their work. Finding the right balance between necessary and sensible adaptations on the one hand, and individual design expression on the other, is one of the most challenging aspects of preparing designs for existing buildings. Attention to detail is the measure of success or failure, and it is unfortunate that, all too often, insufficient care is taken during this somewhat unloved planning phase, causing an ambitious design to slip back into mediocrity. Such pitfalls may be easily avoided by accepting some fundamental prerequisites, and by adopting a limited number of basic principles that apply to the design and planning of construction works in existing buildings.

PREREQUISITES

Development not demolition

Historic building materials have demonstrated their longevity through their very survival across many decades or even centuries. In many respects they show themselves superior to modern building materials. Given this, it is both surprising and distressing to observe that largely intact buildings are often stripped down to their basic construction, only to be restored to their preceding condition again using modern materials. This not only destroys items of potential national, cultural and historical value, but also deprives others of the chance to utilise and exploit the potential of historic buildings, an aspect of increasing importance in the property market. It is precisely the qualities of craftsmanship that many owners or potential buyers value in old buildings. The individual character of historic glazed windows, the complexity and craftsmanship of stucco elevations or the ornate decorative ceilings of historic rooms are difficult to regain if lost due to carelessness

*Questa immagine di memoria conservata, da proteggere è per me la misura di riferimento.

Exacting repair of a window: only the damaged sections have been repaired.

during the construction process. The artistic and technical merits of the architect's design stand or fall with his or her ability to bring out the existing qualities of the building, and to supplement them with contemporary additions. Therefore, although it is often laborious, it is important that the preservation of the existing building substance takes priority over demolition work. This should be adhered to not only in principle but also considered carefully in detail, with an evaluation of whether each building measure is sensible.

An element-for-element approach
The design of new buildings can often be reduced to a collection of repeatable, standardised details. In principle, architectural design for existing buildings does not depart from this approach: where new elements are added or where similar requirements recur, the repeated use of common details can impart a degree of consistency to an otherwise often chaotic building project.
That said, a fundamental principle when developing plans for existing buildings is that the design and planning should be adapted to fit the specifics of the existing building rather than forcing a standardised approach on the building. For example, wall openings that at first appear to have the same dimensions will upon closer examination invariably differ in size. It follows that although the windows appear to be of the same size, the

Plan of works for strengthening the roof construction in Castelvecchio, Verona, by Carlo Scarpa. Original scale 1:10.

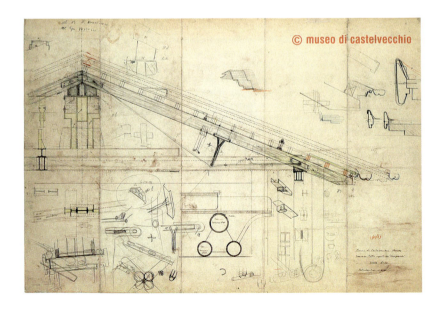

architect must stipulate each of the window dimensions precisely. Leaving this to the contractor may otherwise result in the smallest dimension being used, with the inevitable result that the larger openings will have chunky frames. Cases such as this demonstrate that it is insufficient to develop a series of standard details for an existing building. Indeed, in most instances it will be necessary to create a drawing for each individual situation, showing not only the design and technical solution but also how it can be realised in that particular physical location. The plans of individual works must therefore take into account their physical context, where necessary drawing it in three dimensions.

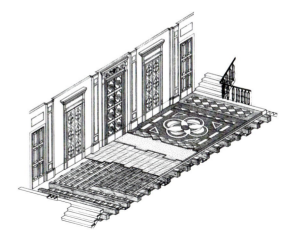

Analytical drawing of the Teatro Giuseppe Verdi in Pisa, by Massimo Carmassi.

Every new building measure and every new building element impacts on the existing building somewhere. The point at which old and new meet should be designed deliberately and systematically, and should be detailed in a drawing. In the past builders traditionally employed a wide variety of details for such transitions including fillets, cover strips, mouldings and recesses, many of which are largely forgotten today. Modern building construction is too often given to using mastics and sealants to cover joints, and not all architects give adequate consideration to such details. The principles that apply for newly inserted building elements are equally valid for renovation work. In complex cases, it may even be necessary to develop detailed drawings for what may at first appear only to be minor and limited damage. The architect should not leave the selection of appropriate repair works and their extent to the contractor, just as he or she would not delegate architectural design decisions. Again, the only reliable basis for planning is one that considers each building element individually.

Repair of rafters: only those sections that are actually damaged are cut out of the rafters and replaced.

The reading room in the covered courtyard.

The modern roof is separated from the surrounding buildings by a glazed strip.

The even walls of the courtyard elevations are painted with jambs around the windows and fake conservator's finds as an ironic reference to the history of the building.

Floor plan of the library complex.

A current representation of historical finds

Library, 1625 / 1980
Eichstätt, Germany
Client: University of Eichstätt
Architect: Karljosef Schattner

Built in 1625 and altered in 1688, the Ulmer Hof was built as a canonical residence and later converted for use as a library for the University of Eichstätt. The courtyard was roofed over to create space for the reading room. The historic dimension of the complex is recorded on the courtyard elevations in the form of fake "conservator's finds" painted in an enlarged and generalised form onto the wall, an ironic reference to the building's history. By contrast, much of the original substance was lost when the building was gutted for conversion.

The modern additions differentiate themselves from the old and smoothened building fabric in material and surface finish. The new elements are separated from the existing fabric by a joint and by a broad glazed strip at roof level.

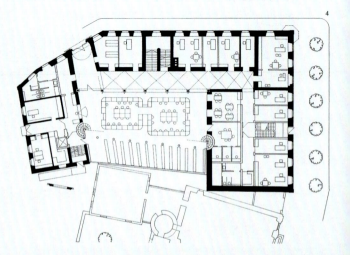

Planning on the basis of an accurate measured survey

In many situations, following the approach above would not be feasible without an accurate measured survey; it is usually a false economy to work solely from schematic plans. A measured survey that is true to deformations is the only reliable basis for detailed construction planning, especially when buildings exhibit deformations or irregular shapes. If the floor slopes, the direction in which a door opens can be an important criterion: if disregarded, it may be necessary to cut an unsightly section out of the door. The decision to apply a new levelled floor over an uneven floor, if not thought through adequately, may result in an uncomfortably low sill height beneath the windows, and in the worst case this may no longer even conform to safety regulations for railing height.

If architects are unaware of walls and floors which are inclined or slanting, or do not pay close attention to this when planning, unfortunate discoveries can arise at construction time, especially when new interventions span several storeys as is the case with stairs, lifts, chimneys and service ducts. It can be a nasty surprise to discover during construction that a new intervention will not fit, because structural elements of the old building are unexpectedly found to be "in the way". Where this may be an issue, it is advisable to draw sections through all necessary axes of the planned construction to establish vertical relationships in advance, or to undertake 3D laser scans to ensure that the planned intervention will fit.

An accurate measured survey is essential wherever repairs or alterations are to be undertaken in historically or technically complex situations. Exact plans which accurately describe the planned measures, their extent and execution are the only reliable basis for successful construction works. It is the relationship between technical improvements and the conservation of artistic values and historic fabric that presents the greatest challenge to the planner and demands the greatest level of planning detail.

Finally, one should also be aware that the irregularities of an old building, whether built that way or distorted through age, will result in difficulties when attempting to introduce modern building products, which are generally precisely cut and perfectly straight. One can, of course, solve this problem with malleable filler materials or elastic mastics. Aside from reservations about using these from a conservation point of view, such slapdash approaches rarely result in good architectonic solutions.

Plans for the renovation and completion of a partially damaged natural stone door jamb. The basis is a measured drawing showing deformations and incorporating all recorded information, e.g. plaster and paint analyses. The success of the planned measures is dependent upon an exact element-for-element specification. Analytical drawing of the external face (original scale 1:20), plan of works for the internal face and completed condition.

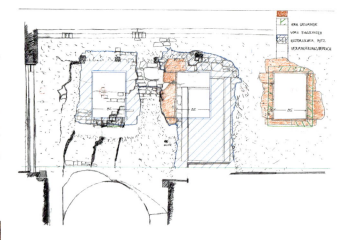

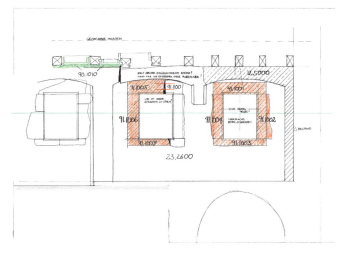

Where old and new meet, transitions and adaptations should be considered and planned with care from the outset, obviating the need for spontaneous on-site decisions or complicated technical solutions.

Adjustable bolts, easily adaptable cover strips or wood blocks cut to size are just some tried and tested solutions, but the appropriate solution should be considered for each situation afresh.

Principles

In addition to conforming to generally accepted standards and building regulations, the detail planning of works should adhere to a few additional basic principles, which result from the fact that constructions and materials are largely set before construction works begin. The opposite approach of designing according to a system that ignores the building and such principles will almost certainly lead to incalculable problems, cost overrun and delays.

The floor joist has been trussed with sag rods. The load is transferred via four bolts in the lower base plate.

Repair not renew

Every old building will exhibit wear and tear after decades of use and exposure to wind and weather. As a result, the planner may feel inclined to renew worn building elements. However, they may still be able to serve their purpose for a long time, and it is always worth first examining whether worn elements can be repaired. This is not only better from an ecological point of view; in many cases it is also much more economical. One should also consider that existing building elements are usually exempt from current regulations, whereas new building elements will have to conform. This is just one of the reasons why a comprehensive conversion can often be more effective than erecting a new building.

Repair in this context should only mean REPAIRS. This in turn means that the intervention should be limited to what is absolutely necessary. The use of the same tools and the same materials that craftsmen used in the past ensures that the entirety of the construction remains homogenous – an important precondition for problem-free construction. Special attention should be

Traditional conservation-oriented strategies also prove their worth in "standard situations" and are often more economical than replacement. Backfilling of cavity behind render from around 1900.

given to the APPROPRIATE CHOICE OF MATERIALS for repairs. Plasters and renders, for example, are usually mixed especially to match the colour and structure of the surrounding area. A degree of careful experimentation and several sample panels may often be necessary to achieve the right recipe. These must be given due consideration during the construction process.

Similarly, the choice of suitable mortars and pointing for old brickwork should not be left to the contractor or blindly follow technical regulations. Before voids are filled or pressure-grouted, an analysis of the existing mortar is essential. Unsuitable mortars may result in ettringite formation and expansion of the mortar, pushing the brickwork apart. Cement mortars cannot be applied where lime mortars have previously been used. Intact brickwork dissipates excess moisture in the construction through the mortar bedding, and if the joints are sealed with an impervious material such as cement mortar, the moisture is forced into the brickwork itself, ultimately damaging it. Cement mortar is therefore almost always inappropriate for old brickwork. Weathered or washed out mortar indicates that the hardness of the mortar was correctly chosen. Mortar joints should be regarded as a wearing layer that protects the more valuable masonry. Care should therefore be taken to ensure that new materials are compatible with the existing construction. The large number of renovation problems and subsequent damage that can result from insufficient knowledge of the existing building should serve as a warning to the planner.

Finally, from a formal and aesthetic point of view, the continuation of a tradition in terms of materials is also advisable where building elements need to be replaced in their entirety, even though in principle a number of alternatives would be possible. Plastic windows with chunky profiles, however practical or supposedly durable they may be, do not fit in a historic building. Vinyl wall coverings or the like are not only vapour impervious; they also destroy any historic atmosphere. Similarly, brick slips do not belong on buildings built before 1920.

A cumulative process

Any building measures undertaken in or within an old building are unlikely to be the last in its long history. The notion that a design is "once and for all" and will last forever is naïve, not only in today's fast-moving day and age. Indeed, renovation and conversion works would not be necessary if structures never deteriorated and if standards of fittings never became obsolete. As such, repairs and additional fittings are to be expected. Given this, the question is how to design adaptations to existing building structures so that these too can, in their turn, be adapted at some point in the future to meet the economic and living requirements of the age.

And when repairs are necessary, this does not automatically entail the removal and replacement of damaged or weakened building elements. Such "repairs" can often snowball, leaving little of the original building substance remaining.

Newly introduced building elements do not have this disadvantage. The correction of deficits through additive building measures which at least in theory are reversible and which conserve the original identity of the historic building has a long tradition. That this tradition can be traced back to the 19th century historic preservation movement does not question its validity in the slightest. On the contrary, such strategies are as applicable as ever, both in general and in detail. *"Better a crutch than a lost limb"* notes John Ruskin succinctly in his *Seven Lamps of Architecture* published in 1849. In addition to the obvious advantages from the point of view of conservation, such measures are usually also less costly. That new interventions are plainly recognisable as being of their time gives them a special quality of their own. This approach comes close to being a reversible measure, one that leaves the original building untouched and introduces a new use in such a way that it can be removed without great cost to the original structure. In practice it is clear that no building works can be absolutely reversible. Yet there is a large difference between a heavy concrete construction that necessitates fundamental interventions in the building structure and other solutions that are easier to remove at a later date.

The occasionally somewhat relaxed approach to structural dimensioning in the past and the higher load and safety requirements stipulated in today's regulations often make it necessary to strengthen the load-bearing capacity of old structures. The most obvious approach is to replace the weak structural member with one of sufficient structural stability. However, the collat-

The town walls in Visby were protected against collapse in the mid-19th century using cast-iron columns - simple and effective.

eral damage that the removal and replacement of structural elements entails rules out such measures in almost all cases.

ADDITIONAL STRUCTURAL SUPPORT is a better and more economical strategy. The load-bearing capacity of insufficiently dimensioned ceiling joists can be compensated for by the addition of a binding beam in midspan: this simple measure reduces the necessary cross-section of the joists drastically, often obviating the need for any other strengthening measures. The burden placed on a column can be reduced by placing an additional post adjacent to it. Openings in walls can be filled in to improve the structural stability of walls, and flanges can be used to stabilise overloaded bearing elements. Additional rafters placed between existing rafters will reduce the load each rafter has to bear. Delicate cable trussing can improve the load-bearing capacity of a binding beam, and in extreme cases, can be used to stabilise vaulting. Last but not least, slender tension rods can be used to take up the load that may be pushing walls apart.

Similar principles apply for BUILDING SERVICES. In most cases modern requirements and the prevailing technical standards will necessitate the complete renewal of the building's services. The insertion of concealed wiring beneath plaster results in systematic damage throughout the entire building, often at considerable cost. Again, additive measures represent a cost-effective and conservation-oriented alternative. By deliberate routing wiring on the wall rather than in the surface of the wall, damaging interventions can be avoided.

Also in this case the architect will have to plan these measures in more detail than normal: each specific situation for each set of wires will need to be planned, and detailed solutions will inevitably need to be developed. However, this approach in most cases is best for the building and for the appearance of the overall result.

A further commonly used and useful additive measure is the lining of walls with murals, wall coverings, stucco details or other "finds" in the building with a SECOND SKIN in order to protect them from further wear and tear. It

Twice the effect: structural repair and building a museum

Naumburg City Museum, 1991–1999
Naumburg, Germany
Client: Naumburg Town Council
Architect: Johannes Cramer

A catwalk in the roof mounted on a horizontal steel truss.

The structural stability of the pitched roof from 1531 had been compromised by the incorrect removal of the tie beam some decades ago. The external walls had bowed outwards and cracked and some rafters had broken under the load. Others were damaged by beetle infestation. The renovation concept retained much of the original building substance including the roof in its existing form. The structural and thermal function of the roof is fulfilled by a new steel roof structure, an additive measure inserted over and between the existing roof. A steel truss was inserted horizontally just above the ceiling joists and runs at a slight diagonal across the floor plan, serving both as a 'catwalk' in the roof and to stiffen the lateral forces. New exposed ventilation ductwork was introduced above the old collar beams.

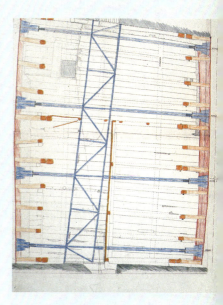

Execution drawing showing the position of the horizontal steel truss.

View up into the ridge with exposed ventilation ductwork.

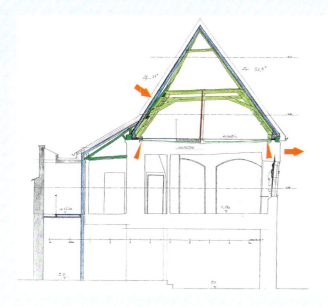

Cross section as an accurate measured drawing with analysis of the supporting structure and schematic representation of the structural solution.

The visible routing of cables under the ceiling avoids damaging the existing building fabric and has an aesthetic appeal of its own: London, Tate Modern (Herzog & de Meuron, 2000).

Not only for old buildings – cables routed visibly along the ceiling in modern architecture: Kunsthal in Rotterdam (Rem Koolhaas, 1992).

is, of course, possible to restore and present such finds; however, this is not a legal requirement and protective measures may be the simplest, least costly and best way to preserve the finds for the future. Whether the second skin is a freestanding construction or anchored to the wall is secondary, as long as the finds themselves are not damaged.

The need to improve the energy efficiency of buildings has consequences for the external skin of a building. Contrary to popular belief, the overall energy performance of an old building, particularly when heavy in mass, is much better than is generally believed.

The common solution of applying a layer of external insulation most often unpleasantly disfigures the appearance of the building. Many architects have solved this problem by introducing a second skin outside the building. As with the structural measures described above, the strategy is not to upgrade an existing built substance, but to resolve its deficits using an additional building element. The "bell jar" approach often associated with conservation projects is rarely successful, as can be seen in the new building on the Pariser Platz in Berlin (Behnisch/Durth) which incorporates the ruin of the Akademie der Künste within an entirely new building. The alternative approach of locating the second skin within the existing building, forming a climatic buffer zone inside the building for access and services, borrows principles from modern climatic glazing façades and has proven successful for many old buildings.

Reclaimed materials

The material and aesthetic quality of many historic building materials is undisputed. Old brickwork and roof tiles exhibit subtle variations in colour, panelled doors and deep profiled architraves bestow buildings with their own particular atmosphere, and the natural irregularity of old floorboards is difficult to emulate – even if the owner is willing and can afford it. Given this, it is hard to understand why old and still functional building materials end up in the skip only to be replaced by almost identical but new materials.

The freestanding shelves made of Cor-ten Steel give the sacral space a special character: Toledo, cultural centre (Angeles Novas & Fernando Barredo, 2004).

The new insertions into this school building in Berlin are completely independent of the load-bearing structure and lend the room a totally different character (Die Baupiloten, 2003).

Each storey has a character of its own.

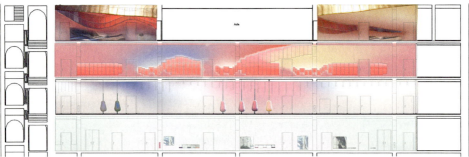

The lecture theatres at the University of Applied Sciences in Wildau, Germany, are autonomous elements built inside a former factory, each with their own structure and services. The factory façades remain largely unchanged (Anderhalten, 2007).

A timber-clad country cottage with its gable cut off is housed within a new glazed construction (Meixner/Schlüter/Wendt, 2004).

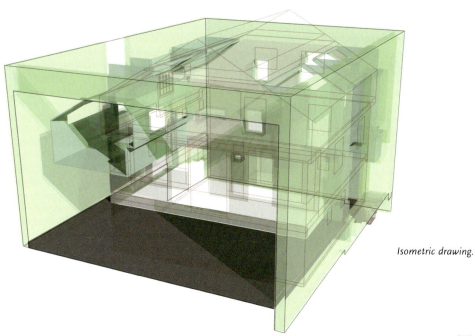

Isometric drawing.

With this in mind, a responsible planner will want to identify all possibilities where existing building materials can be re-used, and whether and to what degree the use of old building materials is appropriate to the project aims. The recovery of such materials is by definition more costly and requires additional planning. The architect must determine in each case which elements are to be salvaged, by what methods, and where and how they will be stored before being re-used. From the point of view of workload, it would be simpler to specify gutting and disposal, and the temptation to cut corners is obvious; nevertheless the easier option inevitably leads to a poorer end result. Aside from considerations of sustainability, the re-use of old building materials is not only aesthetically more authentic, but often also more economical for the client.

Where building materials recovered from the site are not sufficient for the building measures planned, a flourishing trade in salvaged materials may be able to provide additional matching material for almost all historic building materials. From bricks of all formats to floorboards, hinges and door handles, one can find almost everything with a little initiative.

New building made of old bricks. The patina lends the building a particular character: Museum Island Hombroich by Erwin Heerich.

The re-use of recovered roof tiles; checked carefully upon removal, stored on end and covered, each is just as good as a new tile.

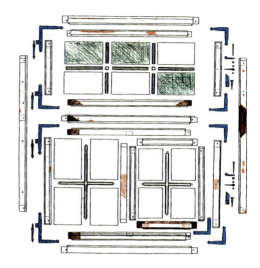

Precise documentation of damage to a timber window.

Solutions: two examples

This book is not meant as a manual for the renovation of old buildings. The following, however, are good examples of how an analysis of defects, possible repair strategies, and the resulting built solution are interlinked. The underlying principles are transferable to other questions not dealt with in detail here.

Upgrading the thermal performance of windows

The removal of "old and draughty" wooden windows and their replacement with plastic thermal windows is a common strategy for modernising and improving the energy efficiency of old buildings even though a systematic analysis of defects often shows that the technical defects of existing windows are comparatively minor. In many cases, the windows could be repaired for a fraction of the price of replacement; however, single-glazed windows have a number of clear disadvantages: they are draughty and offer poor thermal and noise insulation. All of these deficits can be alleviated simply and cost-effectively through additive measures. Furthermore, the original historic window can be retained. The addition of a second layer of windows, connected to the original windows by a box frame, dramatically improves the noise insulation and renders thermal insulation acceptable. The latter can be improved by using thin (10mm) thermopane glazing for the internal window panes, while a lip seal ensures the windows are draught-proof. Known as "Kastenfenster",

After renovation and modernisation: a shady balcony is built over to provide two new bathrooms.

Saving building materials from the skip: preserving identity by reusing existing elements

Villa, 1997
Buchschlag, Germany
Client: private
Architect: Johannes Cramer

A typical villa built in 1912 was to be converted to the modern needs of a family whilst maintaining as much of its historical identity as possible. Two new bathrooms, until then lacking, were added by building on top of the shady balcony on the north elevation. Its timber construction echoes the grey tree trunks of the beech trees in the garden. Defects were repaired throughout and elements which were no longer adequate for their purpose were upgraded using additive measures instead of replacing them. Where walls were demolished, the windows and doors were first carefully removed and used elsewhere in the building. For the insulation of the roof, the roof tiling was taken up, stored and then re-roofed, missing areas being completed with reclaimed roof tiles.

Upgrading building elements: a second inner layer strengthens the door and provides a new locking mechanism and alarm system.

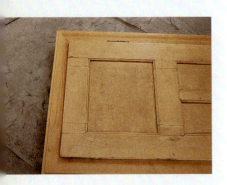

A panelled door is adjusted to fit into another opening in the same house.

Building elements change position: drawings submitted as part of the planning application showing the re-utilisation of existing elements.

or "box-window", this kind of window was commonly used in buildings from the turn of the century and can be seen throughout central Europe. As this additive measure obviates the need for almost all ancillary works associated with the removal and replacement of windows, this approach is almost always more economical, and is aesthetically more authentic. The "disadvantage" is that it necessitates extra planning and coordination – the extra effort is recommended nonetheless in the interests of sustainability.

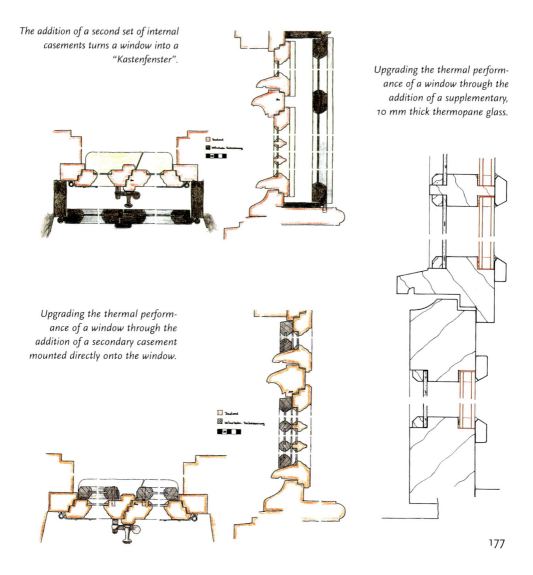

The addition of a second set of internal casements turns a window into a "Kastenfenster".

Upgrading the thermal performance of a window through the addition of a supplementary, 10 mm thick thermopane glass.

Upgrading the thermal performance of a window through the addition of a secondary casement mounted directly onto the window.

Repairing timber roof structures

Timber constructions such as roofs or half-timbered buildings can last many hundreds of years provided they are kept dry and are protected from water ingress. Contrary to popular belief, beetles, woodworm and other pests do not present a major threat to historic timber constructions. There are only very few beetle larvae that can feed on dry wood. For this reason, green and moist softwood timbers are most at risk; fresh infestation of old timbers is the exception. Even in such cases, only the sapwood is affected, whilst the heartwood remains intact – even when the surface damage looks dramatic, the structural stability of the timber may not be affected. The most serious damage is caused by persistent dampness over time. Continually high moisture content levels will lead to rot within the wood and the subsequent loss of tensile strength. In moist and unventilated conditions, timbers may also become infested with dry rot fungus. With time, dry rot will cause systematic wood decay and its mycelium strands are able to penetrate large distances through non-wood materials in its search for suitable conditions. Dry rot is vulnerable to higher temperatures (above 27°C) and below a temperature of 20°C it falls dormant, though it will become active as soon as favourable climatic conditions prevail. It is therefore important to eradicate dry rot entirely. In both cases, a detailed TIMBER INFESTATION APPRAISAL should be carried out by a qualified professional. The report details the extent of fungal attack and the constructions affected, for example charting damage to each of the rafters and determining the remaining load-bearing cross-section through tapping, endoscopy or drilling resistance measurement. In addition, all decay (beetle infestation and fungal attack) will be charted according to type and extent,

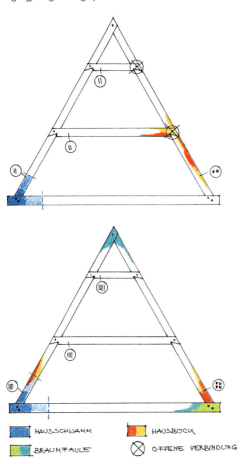

Charting damage in the roof construction: precise detail survey of damage for two pairs of rafters exhibiting differing damage patterns.

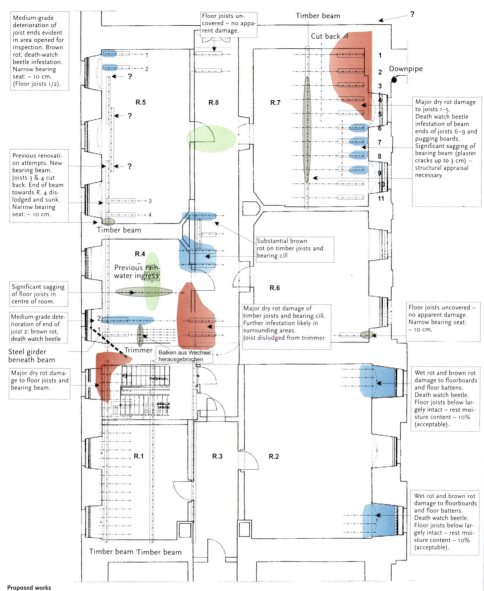

Repair of damage to the base of the roof construction in Oettingen town hall, Germany. The expert craftsmanship of the carpenter has its own character, informed by history. (Reuter + Mittnacht).

pattern of damage, fruiting bodies and spores, and may also be classified with the help of subsequent laboratory investigations. The appraisal will also recommend measures necessary to eliminate the problem. Even if the architect decides not to follow all the recommendations provided, a systematic timber infestation appraisal provides indispensable information, particularly for load-bearing timber structures. The appraisal will also indicate if treatment with hazardous wood preservatives and insecticides has been undertaken previously. If such substances are detected (Hylotox/Xylamon), workmen may need to use protective breathing apparatus.

The appraisal forms the basis for determining the detailed measures required for the repair and, where necessary, the strengthening of the roof construction. In the simplest case this may entail the replacement of damaged sections by qualified craftsmen.

Where there are many cases of similar damages, each should be remedied in turn applying the same repair methods. In such cases the extent of each instance of the damage determines the degree of repair or replacement necessary. Exacting work is required of the craftsman for both technical and aesthetic reasons.

Occasionally, additional structural supporting measures may be necessary, either to rectify deficiencies in the roof structure or to conform to stricter regulations or increased loads. A precise plan of damages and a measured drawing that shows all deformations are an essential basis, especially when strengthening measures are necessary.

Repair of damage to the base of the roof construction in Oettingen town hall. The expert craftsmanship of the carpenter has its own character, informed by history. (Reuter + Mittnacht).

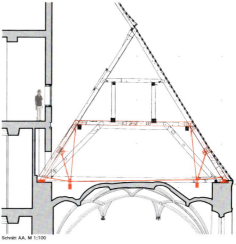

The base of the roof structure of the Heiliggeistchapel in Berlin, exhibiting extensive damage. An additional steel construction is introduced to stabilise the system without damaging more of the building fabric (Hüffer/Ramin, 2005).

Further reading

Only limited general literature on this topic is available. A basic introduction can be found in FEILDEN and WHELCHEL. GROSSMANN 1994, HÖLSCHER and LIPP describe general repair strategies and the implementation is described by KLOTZ-WARISLOHRER. AHNERT/KRAUSE or MANUALE DEL RECUPERO provide systematic drawings of historic building constructions. BECKMANN and PIEPER describe the particular issues associated with historic load-bearing structures.

GRÜN and REUL offer helpful advice on strategies in the context of historic materials.

As a general guide to questions of renovation, RAU/BRAUNE and BAUEN IM BESTAND offer further extensive literature on specific issues. The renovation of timber structures is described in TAMPONE 1996 and 2002 as well as by RIDOUT. KÖNNER and GROSSMANN 1994 offer extensive information on the durability of historic constructions.

A general overview of typical damage patterns for common constructions together with the necessary investigation and repair methods is given by REUL. WENZEL/KLEINMANN's series of volumes with practical recommendations on the conservation of historic buildings provides detailed information on historic masonry, mortars, steel and iron constructions, timber constructions and foundations.

BUILDING WORKS

It is precisely because history should be continued that it is so important to consider how the new should be and how it should relate to what already exists.* Karl Friedrich Schinkel

SITE FACILITIES

The on-site facilities for construction projects on vacant sites have different requirements and organisational arrangements to those for projects involving existing buildings. The improvement and development of existing buildings involves not only ensuring that contractors work with great care, but also that the existing building fabric is not damaged or demolished through carelessness or ignorance. The transport of materials, their storage, the entrances, access routes and common areas all need careful planning and organisation. Furthermore, from day one of building works, built elements already exist on site, items that may be valuable and therefore liable to theft. The building site has to be secured appropriately and kept locked when building works are not in progress. By observing these few basic principles, many unnecessary problems during the building works can be avoided.

The building site as a public attraction

Building sites are often objects of fascination for the general public. Famous building sites such as Ground Zero in New York or the Potsdamer Platz in Berlin, with its "Infobox", have always been and still are a public attraction for passers-by and future users alike. Construction work on existing buildings is especially fascinating, offering sights of interest right from the start of the work. Many of the individual building measures are of a small scale and exhibit skilled craftsmanship, and as such are well-suited to public display. This can take the form of regular opening times, of "open days", or of suitably secured paths through the building site. In all cases the safety regulations must be observed and it is wise to exclude the owner's liability should accidents nevertheless occur.

In general, the building site will be much more informative to the public if it is supported by an occasional guided tour or by descriptive signs, boards or plaques, even if these are makeshift. Archaeologists have a long tradition of communicating their work, and their experience offers good pointers to how this can be achieved.

*Aber eben dadurch, dass die Geschichte fortgesetzt werden soll, ist sehr zu überlegen, welches Neue und wie dies in den vorhandenen Kreis eintreten soll.

The complete enclosure of the building site is the only way to ensure that works can progress independently of the weather.

Stone restoration work on a fountain in Trient, Switzerland, is open for public viewing every afternoon. Descriptive panels explain the building works.

"You are entering the year 1600" – presenting the building site to the public as part of an open day.

Direct contact is the only way for the participating decision makers to fully understand the complex interrelationships in a building.

The history of a building can also be an attraction after building measures have been completed: conserved wall; finds from the house and a chronology describe the historical dimension.

The workshop principle

Well-ordered, conservation-oriented and sustainable site management can only succeed if all participating workmen are aware that building works in existing buildings have more in common with a workshop environment than a construction site. This can sometimes literally mean that an entire building is enclosed in a temporary cover for the duration of the building works – that the building is brought into the workshop, in a manner of speaking. This principle has proven effective over decades of conservation work, and is now often used also for comparatively ordinary buildings. It affords protection from wind and rain, protecting finished work from damage through sudden showers, and allowing work to progress unhindered. Temporary on-site heating measures can enable work to continue regardless of outdoor temperatures.

Temporary air conditioning protects extensive areas of exposed decorated walls and ceilings from damage during the building works.

A well-ordered building site is an essential aspect of the workshop principle. Chaotic conditions where building materials are stacked messily, building rubble is not removed and works progress haphazardly will impede the work of even the best workmen, and may result in unintentional or thoughtless damage to intact parts of the existing building. The site supervisor should ensure that the building site is kept orderly and cleared regularly, just as a workshop would be.

An environment conducive to concentrated work will encourage workmen to use their tools with the same care and attention to detail as they would in a workshop, and accordingly to achieve better results. Where chaotic conditions prevail, good results cannot be expected.

Protective measures for building elements on site

The protection of the existing building fabric, whether in good condition or awaiting further building measures, is one of the central tasks for the site

The uncontrolled dropping of rubble throws an entire building site into disarray.

A tidy building site motivates tradesmen to work exactingly and with respect for the existing building fabric, in Villa Mosler by Mies van der Rohe.

supervisor. The building industry is used to working from the building shell to fitting out, and contractors will need to be made aware that when working within existing buildings large parts of the building fabric are already in a usable or near-usable condition, and should stay that way. Nonetheless, all too often intact rooms do end up being damaged during the building process and for this reason, it can often be advisable to close off entire sections of buildings, and to ensure and check that they remain closed off. This will only be effective if closed-off areas are designated as such and are clearly marked.

Protection measures range from shielding areas where materials are transported in the building and where accidental damage is to be expected to protecting especially sensitive areas that may suffer damage from vibrations or moisture ingress. Experience shows that architects are invariably over-optimistic about the care that can be expected from contractors in their attempt to fulfil their quotas quickly and efficiently. Among the areas most vulnerable to damage are the routes into and through the building along which materials and equipment will be transported. Protective sheathing should be provided around doors and entrances and protective floor panelling laid on vulnerable floor surfaces, taking care to ensure that they do not rub or impact on the surface beneath. It is not uncommon to cover all floors until all major works have been completed. Where structural members are to be

The building site as workshop

Heubach Castle, library and museum, 1991–1997
Heubach, Germany
Client: Heubach Town Council
Architect: Johannes Cramer

The very well preserved fittings of this former seat of nobility (see also p. 74) had to be protected against damage during construction works, even when these involved major repair works to the construction. Protective measures had to be undertaken throughout the building. A protective enclosure sheltered the entire building against the elements and sensitive areas such as the original floors were covered with protective sheathing. The creation of conditions similar to a builder's workshop is the best way to ensure exacting craftsmanship and attention to detail.

Aerial view of the building site and its surroundings.

Protective covering laid over the original floor: chipboard panels on insulation matting.

Building works under protective covering: thorough repair of the roof structure and roofing with recovered tiles.

Mapping of defects and evidence of previons colour schemes.

Securing the access route as well as the building fabric with an additional stair that is robust enough for visitors.

The protection of sensitive plaster surfaces with panels and insulation on a latticework support. To prevent it from vibrating or becoming dislodged, the panels should be screwed in place, never nailed.

Safeguarding historic stucco against spray and debris from foundation works using plastic sheeting; Shielding around door jambs as protection against accidental damage from building machinery.

Protecting the edges of plaster surfaces avoids damage during the building works.

replaced in the vicinity of intact building fabric, the surrounding area should be protected. Particularly vulnerable or valuable wall surfaces have to be entirely covered with panelling and with a layer of vapour permeable insulation. Here it is important to consider works that may take place in these areas and whether it will be necessary to open the panelling to effect repairs. Last but not least, elements of the building that are in danger of collapsing or dislodging should be secured temporarily or else removed and stored for the duration of the works.

SUPERVISING BUILDING WORKS

Without continuous presence on site and permanent supervision of the building works, the project design will not be realised to its full potential. However exact the planning may be, and despite comprehensive documentation, there will always be questions that arise during the building works that can only be solved by the architect. Uncoordinated snap-decisions can often have significant implications for other works which even the best contractors will not be aware of. Furthermore, the temptation to simplify complex details is widespread.

The best way for the architect to ensure that a project design will be realised as intended is by being available on site. It is important to know this in advance and to account for it in fee negotiations. In addition, protective measures will only be effective if they are regularly checked and maintained.

Coordinating contractors

The fact that both major construction works and finishing trades often take place alongside one another during work on existing buildings necessitates a tighter coordination of building measures than is the case with new construction projects. Works must not impinge on or damage one another. To achieve this, it is necessary first to determine what is valuable and what is not – and it is just as essential to brief the contractors on site as it is to describe all works in detail in the specification. Realistically, one cannot assume that the detailed descriptions given in the specification have been communicated fully to each and every workman on site. This is why it is so important to protect vulnerable areas from damage, as described above. Because it is not possible to physically protect everything that is of value, it is equally

Areas of particular value should be clearly marked on site.

A conspicuous sign marks an area with paint dating back to the 15th century.

important to mark any items at risk clearly and conspicuously. Any sign will do, as long as it is understandable, clearly visible and remains in place. Rather than explaining the historic or aesthetic value of the area in question, the message should indicate what the contractors should or should not do, e.g. "Leave untouched!".

Where individual building measures apply to specific areas, the extent of measures should be marked clearly and unambiguously. At what point exactly should a structural member be cut and repaired? Which specific areas of plaster should be removed? Which door (those marked with a sprayed X) should be disposed of? Which wall (the one with a line sprayed along its entire length) should be removed? This is the only way to avoid overzealousness resulting in work exceeding what was originally planned.

It is fundamentally important to coordinate the work undertaken by the different trades. A good network diagram, such as that produced by project management software, or other coordinated works schedules, are useful to coordinate measures with one another. Without due consideration, the danger is that one trade will unintentionally damage preceding work undertaken by another. In particular, the routing of services in historic plaster, all manner of mortise and demolition works, works that span several storeys or adaptations to fit irregularities in the building are often the cause of drastic and unwanted damage resulting in entirely unnecessary setbacks.

Samples, tests and mock-ups

Material samples, colour schemes and the fitting of test specimens have become a common strategy in new buildings: alternative elevation panels are tested before cladding an office building; colour schemes are tried out on the building itself before one is chosen. This is equally if not more important when working with old buildings. Ultimately, the new additions and the old building should suit one another, and it is seldom possible to achieve sufficiently reliable results on screen. In Switzerland it has become common practice to mark the volumetric perimeter of a proposed building measure using a scaffold frame to assess its visual impact on the surroundings. The same principle can be appropriate for visualising additional visible construction elements within an old building. A 1:1 model may be the only sure way to determine whether a deep truss girder will disappear in the lofty heights of a large room or obtrusively disturb the overall character of the room. And even if a particular structural solution has been decided on, it can be worthwhile, particularly for large construction elements, to include the prior construction of a lightweight mock-up and its approval in the specification. The mock-up helps determine that the construction can be installed and fits as planned, and also that elements can actually be transported into the building! Only once this has been tested and approved should the manufacture of the actual element begin. Without such verification, the risk is that a complex and expensive construction element may resist all attempts to fit it into the building, with the unavoidable incurrence of further costs as well as possibly serious damage to the substance of the building.

For building materials, the same principles apply as for new buildings: building materials should never be installed without prior viewing of samples and their approval! The particular historic qualities of old building materials often lead to unsightly and undesirable contrasts with modern building materials, particularly with regard to colours and surface textures. Special attention should be given to paints. As ever fewer contractors mix

Colour trials for the reconstruction of the original colour scheme, based on finds made by conservators on site.

Test installation of a wooden mock-up of a supporting construction to be made of welded steel; the principle is good but it is still too bulky in detail.

their paints on site, it is very important to conduct colour tests beforehand and to approve only the desired results. Again, the extra effort involved in realising the plans as intended can be foreseen, and should be included in the specification accordingly.

Specifications and quantities

The specification of construction works for new projects can fall back on all-inclusive specs, saving the architect the sometimes tiresome task of ascertaining quantities. However, the variety of specific individual solutions coupled with the varying extent of repairs for each individual building element mean that works planned for old buildings may need to be broken down and specified in detail. Every action must be considered and where

Exact specifications for the restoration of the different decoration schemes ensure an interesting design appropriate to the historic substance.

A mock-up construction marks the extent of a new building measure (addition of a lift and dormers) to help assess the impact it has on its surroundings.

appropriate specified individually. This includes, for example, detailing the execution of transitions from new materials to the existing building fabric as a separate, individual task. A logical consequence of such detailed specifications is that the reckoning up of completed works must also be conducted in similar detail. Because repair measures are undertaken only where repairs are necessary, this can result in a series of small areas, each of which needs to be measured individually. The specification should therefore explicitly regulate the billing of small quantities, to avoid incurring standard minimum charges often contained in standard specifications.

The detailed and accurate plans created earlier in the planning process prove their worth when it comes to ascertaining quantities. Where planned works have been detailed in drawings in an appropriate scale, the quantities can be determined directly from the drawing. For example, if the working drawings for the structural repair of an irregularly formed façade are based on a stone-for-stone measured survey and include the exact positions and lengths of masonry pins, the quantities used as given in the specs, then, providing the works are carried out as planned, discussions and arguments about quantities should be unnecessary. A further advantage is that the measured drawings also serve as a record of the work undertaken.

CONSTRUCTION TIME AND COSTING

Building works on historic buildings have the reputation of being incalculable, both in terms of cost and time. Although costs and construction times are commonly exceeded, this need not be so. A comprehensive survey of the building, a design that is sensitive to the existing building and rigorous site supervision will all contribute to a more reliable costing and scheduling of works. Should difficulties nevertheless arise, then it should be remembered that this is not a problem limited to working with old buildings, but one of construction and planning in general. Unfortunately, far too many new building projects are also subject to spiralling costs and long construction delays.

Building costs and cost control

In addition to drawing on one's own experience, a number of tools and cost comparisons exist to assist in the proper and reliable costing of building measures, and once one has familiarised oneself with such tools, they provide a sound basis for calculating the cost of works. An intimate knowledge of the building and its specific structural and technical characteristics together with a full description of the individual design intentions are indispensable. If these are not known in advance, it should be no surprise when the final costs do not correspond to initial estimates. Making design decisions during the building process can be a fascinating way of working. It is of course sometimes unavoidable, as earlier decisions may have to be reconsidered based on what is revealed during the actual construction process. One should, however, be aware that spontaneous decisions do have implications for building costs, whether it is the removal of a wall that was originally to be retained, the uncovering of an interesting find instead of concealing it behind protective cladding, or the unplanned fitting out of spaces. Often it is decisions such as these, made without due consideration, that are the cause of escalating costs.

Element-for-element reconstruction of the badly damaged façade of Neu-Agustusburg in Weissenfels (1694), based on a digital measured survey.

Unpleasant surprises later can be avoided by agreeing any necessary additional measures with the client immediately, through the continual monitoring of costs incurred and, more importantly, by verifying that work is actually planned for in the cost calculation before it is undertaken.

The much discussed issue of whether renovation and modernisation works on existing buildings are cheaper or more expensive than a corresponding new building cannot be answered conclusively. Given the varying conditions of existing buildings, the different standards of fittings and the economics of planning, there are simply too many variables involved.

The factor with the greatest influence on construction costs is without doubt whether the envisaged usage can be fitted into the existing building structure with reasonable interventions. If extensive alterations are necessary, even the most economical and sustainable project plan will be unable to achieve major savings. The ability to weigh up the overall interests of the client alongside the project aims is the actual strategic responsibility of the architect.

Scheduling works

Realistic project scheduling is a particularly challenging aspect of construction, and the programming of works within existing buildings, where the works are often interdependent, is without doubt especially so. A common cause of delays is that traditional materials, as found in the building and used for its repair, are often unsuitable for use during the cold winter months. Moisture ingress, for example when filling voids in walling, should be avoided if there is a danger of frost. Some historic building materials should not be used under certain temperatures – for example, the use of lime as a binding agent or coating is severely limited at temperatures below 10°C. Other measures are time-consuming in summer, for instance where chemical processes take place – the stabilisation of disintegrated stone surfaces or their desalination are examples. Good knowledge of the individual building measures is the best way to avoid unforeseen difficulties.

Architect's fees

The planning work involved when working with historic buildings is without doubt far greater than for new buildings. The preliminary investigations are more extensive, the number of specialists involved is greater, the planning process is more complex, and the site supervision requires more involvement on site. The client should be made aware of this early on. It is a common misconception that a survey requires only slight alterations to become a plan, and should therefore be an integral part of an architect's services. Even if some drawing time can be saved, which is in no way certain, this is more than cancelled out by the additional work required in the planning and construction phases. The element-for-element approach when working with existing buildings results in a large number of bespoke solutions and individual situations that need to be detailed. By contrast, when planning a new building, a single standard detail can clarify a whole series of planning questions.

For this reason all but the most basic of surveys and all architectural research are generally considered to be special services and are often remunerated additionally. Furthermore, the particular complexity of design projects for existing buildings can also be reflected by an additional fee surcharge.

Further reading

Very little further reading is available on this topic. KÖNIG/MANDL bring together an extensive overview of building costs. SCHULZ provides information concerning the organisation of the building site. PETZET/MADER and THOMAS also offer insights into aspects of site supervision.

SUSTAINABILITY

*Sustainable development meets the needs of the present without compromising
the ability of future generations to meet their own needs.*

Brundtland report, World Commission on Environment and Development, 1987

The continued use and development of existing buildings is fundamentally sustainable. Its aim is to maximise the overall lifetime of buildings. It ensures that the effort and investment that was required to originally erect a building can be utilised for as long as possible into the present and future. The issue of the lifetime of a building–and the amount of required or possible maintenance and conversion measures it can undergo during its life– is much easier to assess for existing buildings than for new buildings. A house that has been home to three or four generations, or a former factory now used as a space for events or as a fashionable shopping centre, has already demonstrated its ability to adapt to new uses and users. The degree of urban and infrastructural integration and the arrangement, construction and materials of a building have demonstrated their qualities, strengths and weaknesses. The construction has aged, undergone repairs and proved its durability; those elements and materials of the building that were not durable have been replaced. This experience allows one to develop strategies and techniques which guarantee the sustained use of the building long beyond its investment write-off period. With appropriate maintenance, there is no reason why the building cannot progress to future phases of use without the need for major investment. Architectural design in the context of existing buildings extends the use of buildings over multiple future phases of use, and in the process, carries over the existing qualities of the building into the future.

The property market has for a long time been accustomed to taking into account the later use of a building in its calculations. Independent of the different calculation models employed for financing new construction projects, the ability to continue using a building after the amortisation period promises higher returns on the initial investment. The conservation and maintenance of the existing values, the possibilities for conversion, further and interim use and finally the environmentally sound disposal of the building substance are key aspects that can become important economic factors. A building can be understood as a non-recurring investment, whose

*A disgrace for the profession: the thoughtless and unqualified treatment of historic building
fabric leads to unnecessary and costly destruction, robs the historic building of its identity and
makes it impossible for others to use and work with the historic building fabric.*

199

value can be continually increased through appropriate maintenance and clever development.

Facility Management

Facility management is a term used to describe the process of discovering and exploiting the underused resources of existing building stock. It takes into account the entire process of managing buildings and properties across all their operational phases. Particularly for businesses in the manufacturing or service industries, property can often represent a large part of their overall assets. Where these are underused or poorly managed, clever facility management can activate their economic potential. In any case, facility management must be considered in the future business development strategy, if one is to avoid the cost of upkeep from exceeding the utility value of the property.

Facility management begins with the making of an inventory of all properties, their overall value and their function, and draws up a balance of the existing situation. In a second stage, the condition of the individual properties and their optimisation possibilities are assessed. Many approaches and methods are similar to those used for the investigation and surveying of existing buildings for architectural design purposes. Good building plans are once again a must, and the availability of reliable information is a prerequisite for developing strategies of action. The aim of both is to gain added value through the rediscovery and utilisation of pre-existing qualities. The real value of an existing building is of course also dependent upon the way in which one assesses it and how well one communicates this. For this reason facility management must take a step back from the often restrictive conventional notions of valuation and consider how existing property assets can be re-evaluated. In order to obtain a value assessment that is as precise and realistic as possible, the valuation should take into account aspects that are otherwise often ignored. A crucial aspect for the overall calculation is the time span over which a construction project should be assessed. To properly assess the long-term perspective for architecture in the context of existing buildings, one must, of course, take into account costs resulting from a building's operation as well as for repairs and renovation. In this respect, frequent renovation measures will be problematic. When considered over a longer time span, short intervals between renovations can be cost-intensive for several reasons: they fail to fully exploit the usage potential of the renovation measures, they involve some destruction of the existing value of the building, and they incur construction costs for the usable volume which unnecessarily squeeze potential profits.

Design and construction works within existing buildings as well as general maintenance are usually regarded as being expensive. The cost of design in the context of existing buildings is indeed more expensive than their counterparts when erecting a new building. It is important to survey and assess each specific case individually; the cost of individual works can be higher than comparable standard solutions due to the number of bespoke solutions required. The greater proportion of manual labour by qualified craftsmen also increases the costs. When erecting new constructions the costs for materials and labour are approximately equal. This proportion shifts for renovation work: whilst material costs remain relatively low, the cost for labour as well as specialist skills and consulting can amount to as much as 80% of the overall costs. Given this, the aim is almost always to limit the degree of works to the minimum necessary to ensure the continued use of the building, and the overall investment can often be very cost-effective. Although the cost for the design and planning may at first glance appear high, it usually pays for itself as cost savings during the building works.

The cost of construction works for existing buildings is very much dependent upon the building itself and the compatibility of the new usage or requirements. If the new usage is largely compatible and the construction and design intentions are clear in advance, cost savings of up to 40% in comparison to erecting a new building are possible. For certain types of buildings, redevelopment concepts have been developed into successful economic models. Examples are the conversion of inner city former factory buildings into lofts, furniture stores and local centres, or the redevelopment of dockland areas or the fitting out of roof spaces. All these help to strengthen identification with historic building substance, to provide continuity and to contribute to sustainable neighbourhoods.

If one includes the costs for maintenance and repairs in the overall calculation of building costs, which is an integral part of every economic assessment, then sustainable, well-chosen and planned repair, upgrading and conversion works are more cost-effective than new constructions. Finally, the cost for the demolition and disposal of building materials at the end of the useful life of a building should also be part of the overall calculation. Whereas most building materials used before the height of industrialisation are generally easy to recycle and dispose of safely, many more recent building materials from the 20th century either contain hazardous substances, or are difficult to separate from one another, incurring much higher costs for their appropriate disposal.

Monitoring and maintenance

The most cost-effective treatment of existing buildings is continual maintenance and upkeep. Long-term maintenance contracts, regular reviews by caretakers as well as specialists and the keeping of building maintenance logs all support this purpose. The latter documents the ongoing condition of a building over a long period of time, any alterations that have taken place and the development of defects, and provides the necessary basis for recognising and remedying negative developments before they become more serious. Regular and qualified maintenance secures the long-term value, an old insight that is particularly relevant in times of economic constraints.

For the "normal" owner of a historic building, a good model for the sustainable and systematic maintenance of existing buildings is provided by the regular inspections conducted by conservation organisations for culturally important monuments. Housing associations also have long-standing experience in this area. The inspections are usually based on a checklist-based maintenance plan which includes the regular clearance of gutters and downpipes, the repair of leakages and other aspects that can quickly lead to damage to the building fabric. For large buildings such as castles or churches, it has proven effective to conduct building works in phases over an extended period of time so as to be able to observe their impact and sustainability before proceeding with new works. This approach not only spreads the cost of building works over a longer period but also provides maximum feedback for the planner and so contributes to the long-term value of the building.

The use of techniques from facility management enables maintenance, repair, renovation and refurbishment works to be adjusted to fit the actual aging process of the building fabric. The long-term monitoring of an existing building and critical aspects of its construction provides a reliable indication of the aging process of the building and the opportunity to react accordingly. The trick is to undertake as few measures as possible but as soon as they become necessary, so that more serious defects requiring more extensive works can be avoided.

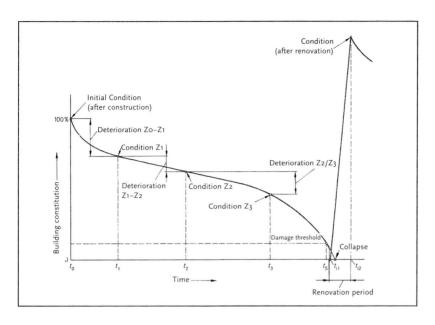

The life cycle of a building and investment in its upkeep. Ongoing maintenance can avoid such major renovation measures; in most cases the standard of the renovation exceeds that of the original building.

Preserving property value

The property market values buildings according to a series of very different factors. Most of these valuation factors are subject to continual fluctuation and include such aspects as advantages and disadvantages of location and the image of the building. The primary task for architects is to ensure that the value of the building is maintained and where possible increased in the long term. Sensitivity is required to find the middle road between conservative preservation and ephemeral fashion. An attempt to increase the value of a property not only by upgrading its standards through the addition of new bathrooms, lifts, insulation etc., but also by remodelling the building according to contemporary tastes, often amounts to short-lived "beautification". The repainting of a façade in more friendly colours or the improvement of the entrance area in an apartment house are without doubt positive for the value of a building; more extensive remodelling can, however, conflict with the overall aesthetic concept of a building or even with its construction. Anyone involved in working on existing buildings should be aware that the long-term value of a building lies in its historic and aesthetic form as embodied by the building fabric. Every alteration will inherently involve some degree of damage to the existing fabric, and this applies equally for alterations to its aesthetic appearance. The post-modern pediment over the entrance to a slab block from the 1960s already appears dated after only ten years. On the other hand, the aesthetics of facing concrete from the 1970s, although presently generally unloved, will probably be more appreciated in the not too distant future.

It is not only cheaper but also maintains the value of a building not to react to short-lived aesthetic fashions and instead to care for and bring out its innate aesthetic qualities. Even aspects which may presently be perceived as passé may be viewed as attractive and exclusive in a few years' time or by other users. As such, architectural design for existing buildings requires not only a whole series of competencies but also and above all, patience.

Further reading:

The approaches and methods of modern facility management are described by GÄNSSMANTEL/ GEBURTIG/SCHAU. ALDA/HIRSCHER provide insights into property development and the valuation of existing buildings. KASTNER details the systematic assessment of historic buildings and the use of checklists. HAMESSE points to the close relationship between economical and ecological renovation strategies. REUL 2005 describes the lack of sustainability and economic absurdity of renovation works planned without thorough knowledge of the building. The development and keeping of building maintenance logs is described by KLEMISCH. He also notes that the care for existing building stock with a view to avoiding more serious damage through the documentation, inspection and specific maintenance of a building is a field that has yet to be fully exploited by architects and engineers. Finally, HASSLER/KOHLER provide statistical information on the existing building stock.

Appendix

BIBLIOGRAPHY

Our selection makes no claim to be complete. The list includes mostly individual publications and indicates which titles architects may find most useful for planning in the context of existing buildings.

AHNERT, Rudolf and Karl Heinz KRAUSE: Typische Altbaukonstruktionen von 1860 bis 1960; Wiesbaden/Berlin 1986

ARENDT, Claus: Modernisierung alter Häuser; Munich 2003

ALDA, Willi and Joachim HIRSCHNER: Projektentwicklung in der Immobilienwirtschaft; Stuttgart 2005

ALMAGRO, Antonio Gorbea: Levantamiento arquitectónico; Granada 2004

ASHURST, John: Conservation of Ruins; Oxford 2007

ASSMANN, Aleida and Dietrich HARTH (Eds.): Mnemosyne. Formen und Funktionen der kulturellen Erinnerung; Frankfurt am Main 1991

ASSMANN, Jan (Ed.): Kultur und Gedächtnis; Frankfurt am Main 1988

BAER, Norbert and Folke SNICKARS: Rational Decision-making in the Preservation of Cultural Property; Berlin 2001

BECKMANN, Paul: Structural Aspects of Building Conservation; London 1995

BEDAL, Konrad: Historische Hausforschung. Eine Einführung in Arbeitsweise, Begriffe und Literatur; Bad Windsheim 1993

BLOOMER, Kent C. and Charles W. MOORE: Body, Memory and Architecture; New Haven/London 1977

BÖTTCHER, Detlef: Erhaltung und Umbau historischer Tragwerke. Holz- und Steinkonstruktionen; Berlin 2000

BOLZ, Thomas and Willem van REIJEN (Eds.): Ruinen des Denkens, Denken in Ruinen; Frankfurt am Main 1996

BOYER, M. Christine: The City of Collective Memory. Its historical imagery and architectural entertainment; Cambridge 1996

BRACHERT, Thomas: Patina; Munich 1985

BRANDI, Cesare: Teoria del Restauro; Milano 1963

BREITLING, Andris and Stefan ORTH: Erinnerungsarbeit; Berlin 2005

BROOKER, Graeme and Sally STONE: ReReadings. Interior architecture and the design principles of remodelling existing buildings; London 2004

CANTACUZINO, Sherban: Re-Architecture. Old Buildings, New Uses; London 1989

CARMASSI, Gabriella and Massimo: Del restauro quattordici case; Milano 1998

CAPERNA, Maurizio and Gianfrancesco SPAGNESI (Eds.): Architettura: Processualità e Trasformazione; Rome 2002

CHOAY, Françoise: L´Allegorie du Patrimoine; Paris 1992

CRAMER, Johannes: Thermographie in der Bauforschung; in: Archäologie und Naturwissenschaften 2, 1981, pp. 44–54

CRAMER, Johannes (Ed.): Bauforschung und Denkmalpflege – Umgang mit historischer Bausubstanz; Stuttgart 1987

CRAMER, Johannes: Bauarchäologie und Entwerfen im profanen Baudenkmal, in: Bauwelt 1988, 33, pp. 1350–1358

CRAMER, Johannes: Handbuch der Bauaufnahme; Stuttgart 1993

DE JONGE, Krista and Koen van BALEN (Eds.): Preparatory Architectural Investigation in the Restoration of Historical Buildings; Leuven 2002

DOCCI, Mario and Diego MAESTRI: Il rilevamento architettonico. Storia metodi e disegno; Bari 1987

ECKERT, Hannes, Joachim KLEINMANNS and Holger REIMERS: Denkmalpflege und Bauforschung; Karlsruhe 2000

ECKSTEIN, Günter (Ed.): Empfehlungen für Baudokumentationen. Bauaufnahme-Bauuntersuchung (= Arbeitshefte des Landesdenkmalamts Baden-Württemberg, vol. 7); Stuttgart 1999

EISSING, Thomas: Zur Anwendung der Dendrochronologie in der Bauforschung: Einige kritische Anmerkungen; in: Bauforschung und Archäologie, eine kritische Revision; Berlin 2005, pp. 297–328

FECHNER, Johannes (Ed.): Altbaumodernisierung. Der praktische Leitfaden; Vienna/New York, 2002

FEHRING, Günter P.: Einführung in die Archäologie des Mittelalters; Darmstadt 1993

FEILDEN, Bernhard M.: Conservation of historic buildings; Oxford etc. 1996

FISCHER, Alfred: Umnutzung alter Gebäude und Anlagen; Stuttgart/Zurich 1992

FISCHER, Konrad (Ed.): Das Baudenkmal. Nutzung und Unterhalt (= Veröffentlichungen der Deutschen Burgenvereinigung e. V. Reihe B, Schriften, vol. 8); Braubach 2001

FRANÇOIS, Etienne and Hagen SCHULZE (Eds.): Deutsche Erinnerungsorte; Munich 2001

FRANZ, Birgit: Behutsame Wiedernutzbarmachung von Bürgerhäusern; Karlsruhe 2003

FRANZ, Eckhart G.: Einführung in die Archivkunde; Darmstadt 1993

GÄNSSMANTEL, Jürgen, Gerd GEBURTIG and Astrid SCHAU: Sanierung und Facility Management. Nachhaltiges Bauinstandhalten und Bauinstandsetzen; Wiesbaden et.al. 2005

GELHAUS, Rolf and Dieter KOLOUCH: Vermessungskunde für Architekten und Bauingenieure; Düsseldorf 1997

GERKAN, Armin von: Grundlegendes zur Darstellungsmethode. Kursus für Bauforschung, 1930, in: Von antiker Architektur und Topographie; Stuttgart 1959, pp. 99–106

GERKAN, Meinhard von: Sanierung und Neukonzeption; Cologne 1988

GIOVANNONI, Gustavo: Il restauro dei monumenti; Rome 1945

GROSSMANN, G. Ulrich: Einführung in die historische Bauforschung; Darmstadt 1993

GROSSMANN, G. Ulrich: 500 Jahre Garantie. Auf den Spuren alter Bautechniken (= Materialien zur Kunst- und Kulturgeschichte in Nord- und Westdeutschland, vol. 12); Marburg 1994

GROSSMANN, G. Ulrich and MICHELS, Hubertus: Fachwerk als historische Bauweise. Ein Materialleitfaden und Ratgeber; Hösseringen 2002 GUIDE to Recording Historic Buildings; Rushden 1990

GUTSCHOW, Konstanty and Hermann ZIPPEL: Umbau (= Die Baubücher, vol. 13); Stuttgart 1932

HAHN, Martin: Historische Umnutzungen; Weimar 2000

HALBWACHS, Maurice: Les cadres sociaux de la mémoire; Paris 1925

HAMESSE, Jean-Elie: Ökologische Bausanierung. Altbausanierung zwischen Ökologie und Ökonomie; Stuttgart/Munich 2001

HASSLER, Uta and Niklaus KOHLER: Umbau, die Zukunft des Baubestands; Tübingen 1999

HERBERS, Jill: Great Adaptations; New York 2005

HÖLSCHER, Martin (Ed.): Das Denkmal als Altlast? Auf dem Weg in die Reparaturgesellschaft; Munich 1996

HOEPFNER, Martina: Ressourceschonendes Bauen durch Umnutzung und Ertüchtigung vorhandener Bausubstanz; Leipzig 1997

HOESLI, Bernhard: Commentary on Colin Rowe; in: Transparency (Robert Slutzky Ed.), Stuttgart 1968, pp. 57–119

HUSE, Norbert: Denkmalpflege, Deutsche Texte aus vier Jahrhunderten; Munich 1996

JENCKS, Charles and George BAIRD (Eds.): Meaning in Architecture; New York 1970

JOKILEHTO, Jukka: A History of Architectural Conservation; Bath 2001

KASTNER, Richard: Altbauten beurteilen, bewerten; Stuttgart 2000

KLEIN, Ulrich: Bauaufnahme und Dokumentation; Stuttgart 2001

KLEMISCH, Jürgen: Bauunterhaltung dauerhaft und wirtschaftlich; Stuttgart 2006

KLOTZ-WARISLOHNER, Gerhard and Martin SAAR: Reparatur in der Denkmalpflege. (= Arbeitshefte des Bayerischen Landesamtes für Denkmalpflege, vol. 101); Munich 1999

KNOPP, Gisbert, Norbert NUSSBAUM and Ulrich JACOBS: Bauforschung. Dokumentation und Auswertung; Cologne 1992

KÖNIG, Holger and Wolfgang MANDL: Baukosten-Atlas, Kissingen 2005

KÖNNER, Klaus and Joachim WAGENBLAST (Eds.): Steh fest mein Haus im Weltgebraus. Denkmalpflege – Konzeption und Umsetzung; Aalen 1998

LAMPUGNANI, Vittorio Magnago: Die Modernität des Dauerhaften. Essays zu Stadt, Architektur und Design; Berlin 1995

LATHAM, Derek: Creative Re-use of Buildings. Vol. 1, Principle and Practice; Shaftesbury 2000

LERCH, Helmut: Wohnhaus-Erweiterungen; Darmstadt 2001

LINHARDT, Achim: Das Umbau-Buch. Neues Wohnen in alten Häusern; Munich 2006

LIPP, Wilfried: Vom modernen zum postmodernen Denkmalkultus. Aspekte zur Reparaturgesellschaft, in: LIPP/PETZET, p. 6–12

LIPP, Wilfried and Michael PETZET (Eds.): Vom modernen zum postmodernen Denkmalkultus? Denkmalpflege am Ende des 20. Jahrhunderts (= Arbeitshefte des Bayerischen Landesamts für Denkmalpflege, vol. 69); Munich 1994

LOEWY, Hanno and Bernhard MOLTMANN (Eds.): Erlebnis, Gedächtnis, Sinn. Authentische und konstruierte Erinnerung; New York 1996

LOWENTHAL, David: The Past is a Foreign Country; Cambridge 1985

LÜBBE, Hermann: Im Zuge der Zeit. Verkürzter Aufenthalt in der Gegenwart; Berlin et.al. 1992

LYNCH, Kevin: What Time is This Place?; Cambridge 1972

MADER, Gert Thomas: Angewandte Bauforschung; Darmstadt 2005

MANUALE DEL RECUPERO del Comune di Roma (Francesco Giovanetti Ed.); Rome 1997

MARTINI, Wolfram (Ed.): Architektur und Erinnerung; Gießen 2000

MASTROPIETRO, Mario (Ed.): Restoration and beyond. Architecture from conservation to conversion; Milano 1996

MATTHEWS, Volker: Vermessungskunde; Stuttgart/Leipzig/Wiesbaden 2003

MEIER, Hans-Rudolf and Marion WOHLLEBEN (Eds.): Bauten und Orte als Träger von Erinnerung. Die Erinnerungsdebatte und die Denkmalpflege; Zurich 2000

MEYER-BOHE, Walter: Bauliche Erweiterungen. Planungshandbuch; Cologne 1997

MÖRSCH, Georg: Denkmalverständnis. Vorträge und Aufsätze 1990–2002; Zurich 2005

MOSCHIG, Guido F.: Bausanierung. Grundlagen, Planung, Durchführung; Stuttgart/Wiesbaden 2004

MOSTAFAVI, Mohsen and David LEATHERBARROW: On Weathering. The Life of Buildings in Time; Cambridge, Mass./London 1993

OSWALT, Philipp (Ed.), Shrinking Cities, vol. 1, Ostfildern 2004

PEDRETTI, Bruno (Ed.): Il progetto del passato. Memoria, conservazione, restauro, architettura; Milano 1997

PETZET, Michael and Gert Thomas MADER: Praktische Denkmalpflege; Stuttgart/Berlin/Cologne 1993

PIEPER, Klaus: Sicherung historischer Tragwerke; Munich 1983

POWELL, Kenneth: Architecture Reborn: The Conversion and Reconstruction of Old Buildings; London 1999

RAU, Otfried and Ute BRAUNE: Der Altbau. Renovieren, Restaurieren, Modernisieren; Leinfelden-Echterdingen 2000

RENFREW, Colin and Paul BAHN: Archaeology. Theories, Methods and Practice; London 1991

REUL, Horst: Handbuch Bautenschutz und Bausanierung. Schadensursachen, Diagnoseverfahren, Sanierungsmöglichkeiten; Cologne 2001

REUL, Horst: Die Sanierung der Sanierung. Grundlagen und Fallbeispiele; Stuttgart 2005
RICŒUR, Paul: La mémoire, l'histoire, l'oublie; Paris 2003

RIDOUT, Brian: Timber Decay in Buildings. The conservation approach of treatment; London/New York 2000

RIEGL, Alois: Der moderne Denkmalkultus. Sein Wesen und seine Entstehung. 1903. In: Gesammelte Aufsätze. Augsburg/Vienna 1929, pp. 144–191

RODWELL, Warwick: The Archaeology of Churches; Stroud 2005

ROSSI, Aldo: L'architettura della città; Padua 1966

RUSKIN, John: The Seven Lamps of Architecture; London 1849

SCHÄDLER-SAUB, Ursula (Ed.): Die Kunst der Restaurierung (= ICOMOS, Hefte des Deutschen Nationalkomitees XXXX); Munich 2005

SCHAFFNER, Ingrid and Matthias WINZEN (Eds.): Deep Storage. Collecting, Storing and Archiving in Art. Exhibition catalogue Haus der Kunst, Munich/New York 1997, pp. 259–261

SCHITTICH, Christian (Ed.): Building in Existing Fabric. Refurbishment, Extensions, New Design; Munich/Basel, Boston, Berlin 2003

SCHLEIFER, Simone (Ed.): Converted Spaces; Cologne 2006

SCHMIDT, Hartwig: Bauaufnahme, die Entwicklung der Methode im 19. Jahrhundert; in: Erhalten historisch bedeutsamer Bauwerke; Karlsruhe 1986, pp. 22–69

SCHMIDT, Wolf: Das Raumbuch als Instrument denkmalpflegerischer Bestandsaufnahme und Sanierungsplanung (= Arbeitshefte des Bayerischen Landesamts für Denkmalpflege, vol. 44); Munich 1989

SCHMITZ Heinz, Edgar KRINGS, Ulrich DAHLHAUS and Ulli MEISEL: Baukosten, Instandsetzung, Sanierung, Umnutzung. Bauinformation Konstruktion und Kosten; Essen 1998

SCHÖFBECK, Tilo: Dendrodaten in der norddeutschen Architekturgeschichte. Methodische Fragen zur Dachwerksdatierung; in: Bauforschung und Archäologie, eine kritische Revision; Berlin 2005, pp. 329–365

SCHRADER, Mila: Bauhistorisches Lexikon: Baustoffe, Bauweisen, Architekturdetails; Hösseringen 2000

SCHULLER, Manfred: Building Archaeology (= ICOMOS, International Council on Monuments and Sites VII); Munich 2002

SCHULZ, Ansgar and Benedikt and Lutz SCHILBACH: Modernisierung von bewohnten Gebäuden. Gestaltung, Technik und Organisation einer neuen Bauaufgabe; Stuttgart/Munich 2001

SCHWEINGRUBER, Fritz H.: Der Jahrring. Standort, Methodik, Zeit und Klima in der Dendrochronologie; Bern 1983

SIMON, Philipp (Ed.): Architectures transformées. Réhabilitations et reconversions à Paris; Paris 1997

SMITHSON, Alison and Peter: The 'As Found' and the 'FOUND'; in: Independent Group. Postwar Britain and the Aesthetics of Plenty (D. Robbins Ed.); Cambridge, Mass./London 1990; p. 201 ff.

SPITAL-FRENKING, Oskar: Architektur und Denkmal. Der Umgang mit bestehender Bausubstanz. Entwicklungen, Positionen, Projekte; Leinfelden-Echterdingen 2000

TAMPONE, Gennaro: Il Restauro delle Strutture di Legno; Milano 1996

TAMPONE, Gennaro: Strutture di Legno. Cultura, Conservazione, Restauro; Milano 2002

TAUSCH, Harald (Ed.): Gehäuse der Mnemosyne. Architektur als Schriftform der Erinnerung; Göttingen 2003

THIÉBAUT, Pierre: Old Buildings Looking for New Use; Stuttgart 2007

THOMAS, Horst (Ed.): Denkmalpflege für Architekten. Vom Grundwissen zur Gesamtleitung; Cologne 1998

TUSSENBROEK, Gabri van (Ed.) and Ronald STENVERT: Bouwhistorie. Opmeten en onderzoeken van oude gebouwen; Utrecht 2007

WAIZ, Susanne: Auf Gebautem Bauen / Costruire sul costruito; Vienna/Bozen 2005

WANGERIN, Gerda: Einführung in die Bauaufnahme; Braunschweig 1986

WEFERLING, Ulrich, Katja HEINE and Ulrike WULFF: Von Handaufmaß bis High Tech; Mainz 2001

WENZEL, Fritz and Joachim KLEINMANNS (Eds.): Empfehlungen für die Praxis (from the SFB 315: Erhalten historisch bedeutsamer Bauwerke). The following volumes have been published: Denkmalpflege und Bauforschung (2000), Historische Eisen- und Stahlkonstruktionen (2001), Baugrund und historische Gründungen (2003), Historisches Mauerwerk (2000), Mauerwerksdiagnostik (2004), Historische Mörtel und Reparaturmörtel (2001), Restaurierungsmörtel (2006), Historische Holztragwerke (1999)

WHELCHEL, Harriet (Ed.): Caring for your historic house; New York 1998

WIEDEMANN, Albert: Handbuch Bauwerksvermessung. Geodäsie, Photogrammetrie, Laserscanning; Basel/Boston/Berlin 2004

WOHLLEBEN, Marion: Bauforschung und ihr Beitrag zum Entwurf (= Veröffentlichungen des Instituts für Denkmalpflege an der ETH Zürich, vol. 12); Zurich 1993

WOLTERS, Wolfgang (festschrift): Der unbestechliche Blick / Lo Sguardo Incorrutibile (Martin Gaier, Bernd Nicolai, Tristan Weddigen Eds.); Trier 2005

WOOD, Jason (Ed.): Buildings Archaeology, Applications in Practice; Oxford 1994

WÜSTENROT STIFTUNG (Ed.): Umnutzung im Bestand. Neue Zwecke für alte Gebäude; Stuttgart/Zurich 2000

INDEX OF ARCHITECTS

ACEA + Comune di Roma 120
Alberti, Leon Battista 9
Anderhalten, Claus 126, 170
Aparicio Guisado, Jesus 150
Asadov, Aleksander 132
Atelier 5 131
Auer, Gerd 23, 153
Augustin + Frank 122
AUIA 132
Aulenti, Gae 123

Baupiloten 142, 172
Behnisch, Günter 171
Bernini, Gianlorenzo 17
Block, Klaus 95, 124
Böhm, Gottfried 119, 126
Bramante, Donato 17
Breitling, Stefan 67, 71
Brouwers, Rob 125
Busse, Hans-Busso von 29

Calatrava, Santiago 105
Canali, Guido 97, 144
Carmassi, Massimo 10, 32, 75, 97, 98, 115, 144, 161
Chipperfield, David 10, 126
Cramer, Johannes 23, 41, 74, 153, 169, 176, 187

Dehio, Georg 21, 48
Diederen + Dirrix 117
Dinse/Feest/Zurl 124
Dixon + Jones 107
Döllgast, Hans 96, 97, 126
Domenig, Günther 156
Donati, Francesca 129

Egeraat, Erick van 100, 109

Fernandez Elorza, Hector 150
Foster, Norman 135, 154, 155, 159
Frotscher, Heinrich 153

Galfetti, Aurelio 10, 98, 135
Gallegos Borges, Gabriel 103
Garcia Delgado, Javier 33
Gehry, Frank 100
Gieselmann, Reinhard 148
Ginsburg, Moisei 30
González, Primitivo 103
Gropius, Walter 21

Harrap, Julian 10, 126
Hänsch, Wolfgang 143
Heerich, Ernst 174
Henket, Hubert-Jan 152
Herzog & de Meuron 10, 20, 170
Hollein, Hans 101, 148
Hüffer + Ramin 181

INNOCAD 132

Jones, Edward 107
Jordi, Marc 134

Kahlfeldt, Petra and Paul 101, 120
Klumpp, Hans 78
Kollhoff, Hans 101, 140, 170
Koolhaas, Rem 100

Lópes Cotelo, Victor 33

Maderno, Carlo 17
MECANOO 100, 109
Meixner/Schlueter/Wendt 173
Michelangelo 9, 159
Miralles, Enric 149
Moore, Charles W. 101
Mozer, Jordan 11
MRJ Rundell + Associates 108
Muzio, Giovanni 95

Neumann, Franz Ignatz Michael 16
Nouvel, Jean 135
Novas, Angeles + Fernando Barredo 171

Ortner, Laurids 102
Oswalt, Philipp 210

Peruzzi, Baldessare 17
Piana, Mario 112
Pitz + Hoh 79
Puente Fernandez, Carlos 33
Purcell/Miller/Tritton 139

Raffael 17
Reuter, Hans 113, 180
Riegl, Alois 21, 210
Ruskin, John 21, 24, 27, 111 167

Sangallo, Antonio da 17
Scarpa, Carlo 10, 97, 98, 116, 143, 144, 145, 159, 160
Scharfetter, Martin 145
Schattner, Karljosef 10, 48, 97, 98, 124, 145, 147, 162
Scherer + Angonese 128
Schinkel, Karl Friedrich 9, 18, 24, 159, 183

Schubert, Leo 112
Schwarz, Rudolf 97
Seelinger, Martin 143
Stirling, James 101

Tesar, Heinz 101

Ungers, Oswald Mathias 147

Valentyn, Thomas van den 137
Venturi, Robert 141

Wehdorn, Manfred 124

Zaanen/Spanjers 104
ZECC Architekten 130
Zumthor, Peter 20

INDEX OF SUBJECTS

Access routes 183, 186, 188
Adaptation 111, 119–134, 139, 164, 165, 199
Addition of storeys 110, 129
Additional structural support 168
Additive measures 41, 88, 116, 167–173, 175
Age, impression of age 21, 116, 138–141
Aging 111
Appropriate choice of materials 166
Archaeology 68, 69, 80, 93, 103
Architectonic expression 120, 137–157, 162, 170
Architect's fees 189, 196
Archives 48–50, 72
As found 99
Authenticity 23, 37
Auxiliary constructions 102, 107, 109, 131

Box window 175, 177
Building archaeology 60, 68-82, 72, 76, 83, 128, 147
Building cost 67, 111, 174, 194–196, 197, 199
Building material 152
Building materials, historic 25, 43, 80, 159, 196
Building mechanics 45, 72, 86–91, 118, 129, 141, 169
Building phase plan 38, 41, 54, 69, 70, 84, 91, 128, 148, 149
Building phases 71, 203
Building plan 54-65
Building record 47, 49, 54
Building rubble 185, 202
Building services 168
Building survey 41, 45, 46, 66–91
Building time 72, 185, 188, 189,194–197
Building works supervision 189–194

Ceiling height 35, 133
Change of use 47, 101, 104, 119, 199
Checklist 46, 53, 202, 205
Circulation 32, 41, 50, 75, 102, 104, 107, 108, 109, 110, 118, 126, 131, 132, 133, 143, 149, 153, 171
Client 34, 35, 40, 102, 147, 174, 196, 202
Combination 132
Completion 126
Composition of building volumes 151
Conservation authorities 37, 40
Conservation 19, 21, 22, 114, 165, 184, 193
Conservation plan 37, 39, 40, 92
Conservation legislation 20
Conservation topographical studies 48

Construction planning 33, 75, 87, 113, 131, 139, 140, 160, 161, 163, 164, 165, 169, 194, 195
Contractors 42, 112, 114, 183, 185, 186, 189–191
Contrast 33, 75, 115, 125, 128, 137, 144, 148, 149, 151, 155, 192
Conversion 126
Corrective maintenance 11, 45, 111–114
Correspondence 100, 115, 117, 127, 137-138, 159
Costing, cost control 193–196, 200, 202
Cultural landscape 18

Dating methods 80, 82
Defamiliarisation 133, 146, 147, 151, 155
Deformation 55, 58, 59, 67, 71, 72, 73, 83, 85, 86, 112, 112, 129, 164
Dendrochronology 68, 81, 93
Design strategies 43, 93, 110

DESIGN STRATEGIES
Adaptation 111, 119-134, 139, 164, 165, 199
Aging 111
Change of use 47, 101, 104, 119, 199
Combination 132
Completion 123
Conservation 20, 22, 114, 165, 184, 193
Conversion 126
Corrective maintenance 45, 111–114
Correspondence 100, 115, 117, 127, 137–138, 159
Modernisation 111, 115–119, 196
Reconstruction 24, 40, 69, 72, 79, 80, 91, 126, 135, 136, 137, 142, 144
Refurbishment 24, 67, 114, 166, 201, 203, 205
Repairs 33, 48, 84, 86, 117, 159, 163, 165, 175, 180, 193, 203
Restoration 111, 114
Upgrading 113, 118, 119 175–177, 180

Detail planning 59, 159–181
Didactic design 146
Digital Building Information System 71
Disposition 101-106, 199
Distortion-rectified photograph 61, 64
Documentation 47, 50–54, 56, 60, 67, 189, 194
Dry rot 30, 178, 179, 180

Edge protection 188
Electrical installation 38, 117
Endangered species, protection of 25
Energy efficiency 36, 118, 142, 170
Exemptions and relaxations 35, 110, 165
Extension 107, 110, 122, 127, 149, 151, 152, 157

Façade 123, 134, 143, 147, 162, 172, 191, 195
Facility Management 54, 59, 93, 200–202, 203, 205
Fire safety 35, 36, 108, 110, 131
Fittings and fixtures 54, 59, 62, 66, 75, 77, 91, 140, 187, 196
Floor plan arrangement 35, 101, 104, 127, 133
Fragmentation 98, 103, 143–147
Functional planning 59, 102–104
Fungal or beetle infestation 86, 178

genius loci 18, 19, 23, 98
Gutting 101, 102, 134, 162

Hand measurement 56, 61, 62
Heating 117, 118, 185
Historic authenticity 23
House-in-house approach 120

Industrial buildings 123, 124
Initial inspection 46
Inspections 202
Interim temporary usage 119
Inventory 48

Joint 150, 151, 153, 162
Junction and delineation 151–157

Laser scanner 58, 62–65, 163
Laser theodolite 58, 61, 62
Lift 41, 58, 110, 125, 133
Listed building 29, 36
Load-bearing capacity 31, 88, 110

Main inspection 46
Maintenance 48, 114, 199, 201, 202–203
Maintenance plan 202
Mapping 46, 91
Marking 47, 53, 69, 190,
Measured survey 41, 44, 53–63, 74, 89
Mock-up 191–192
Modernisation 111, 115–119, 196
Moisture 87, 166, 186
Monitoring 30, 71, 202-203

Noise insulation 36, 175, 177

objet trouvé 99
Opening (sondage) 73, 78, 79

Photogrammetry 61, 62, 93
Photographic record 50
Plan of damages 89, 90, 91
Plan of finds 38, 67

Plan of fittings and fixtures 37, 51, 54, 91
Planning authorities 35–40
Planning detail, degree of 31, 163
Planning permission procedure 37
Planning process 29, 81
Planning, element-for-element 160–163, 197
Precision levels 54–57, 58, 59
Preparatory investigations 31, 45–93, 194
Presentation 98, 103, 144, 145, 147, 155, 157
Preserving property value 202, 203
Property development 199, 204, 205
Protective measures 29–31
Protective measures for building elements 185–189, 190

Reclaimed materials 171–174, 176
Reconstruction 24, 40, 65, 69, 72, 79, 80, 91, 126, 135, 136, 137, 142, 144
Refurbishment 23, 67, 114, 166, 201, 203, 205
Remnant 134
Repairs 33, 48, 84, 86, 117, 159, 163, 165, 175, 180, 193, 203
Restoration 114
Restorer 35, 68, 77–80, 147, 162, 187–193
Reversibilty 37, 167
Roof conversion 127, 130
Room distribution 104
Room log 42, 46, 50, 51, 52, 53, 72

Samples 191-192
Sanitary installation 38, 117
Scanner, 3D: see Laser scanner
Second skin 168, 170
Shadow line 151, 153
Single-glazed window 175, 177
Site facilities 183–189
sotto livello 152, 157
Special services 197
Specifications 54,191, 192, 193
Stairs 33, 41, 58, 105, 108, 116, 121, 162, 163, 188
Standard minimum charges 193
Stereo photogrammetry 61, 65, 78
Strengths and weaknesses, evaluation and interpretation 45, 89–93
Structural stability 84, 88
Structural survey 83–86, 169
Structure 30, 35, 37, 46, 59, 66–72, 84–86, 105, 109, 113, 167, 168, 169, 171, 172, 178, 180, 181, 189
Structured light systems 64, 73

Subdivision 58, 68, 119, 120, 137
Surface-mount installation 117, 121
Survey 54–63, 94, 181, 193, 194
Survey of defects 85, 87, 89, 175, 178
Survey, accurate 53–63, 112, 113, 163
Survey, comprehensive analytical 57, 78
Survey, schematic 55, 195
Survey, tacheometric/geodetic 61, 70, 71
Sustainability 47, 101, 104, 134 165, 174, 177, 159,
   199–205

Thermography 72, 87, 93
Thermopane glazing 175
Timber infestation appraisal 178, 180
Tithe maps 50
Title register 47
Town planning 22

Underpinning 133
Upgrading 113, 118, 119 175–177, 180
User involvement 43

Venice Charter 22, 102

Windows 36, 57, 59, 81, 159, 160, 175–177
Working load 168
Workshop 185, 187
Written information 50, 73, 183, 190

ILLUSTRATION CREDITS

Altenkirch, Dirk 74
Anderhalten, Claus 172
Archivio Museo di Castelvecchio, Verona 160
Atelier 5 131
ASD, Yngve Jan Holland, Andreas Potthoff 63
Augustin und Frank 122

Basel Conservation Department, Hans Ritzmann 56
Basel Conservation Department, Bernard Jaggi 105
Basel Conservation Department, Mathias Merki 56
Basel Conservation Department, Stephan Tramèr 73
Battistella©CISA-A. Palladio, Gianantonio 118
Baupiloten, Susanne Hofmann 172
Bergamo, Fabrizio 206
Berlin Conservation Department 77
Bitschnau/Hauser 128
Bitter, Jan 142, 172
Bleyl, Markus 41, 164, 169
Block, Klaus 124
Blümel, Anke 108
bpk / Kupferstichkabinett, SMB /Jörg P. Anders 17
Braunau City Administration 69
Bryant, Richard / arcaid.co.uk 104

Calatrava, Santiago 105
Carmassi, Massimo 2, 75, 161
Ciampi, Mario 75, 115
Cirenei, Matteo 95
Cramer/Sack 51

Dechau, Wilfried 94
Dienstleistung Denkmal, Semmler/Schmidt 43, 66

Gieselmann, Reinhard 148
Gilbert, Dennis / VIEW 155
Gonzalez, Primitivo 103
Gross, Felix / Kunstverlag Josef Fink 78

Halbe, Roland 123, 150
Helfenstein, Heinrich 105
Hofburg Kongresszentrum &
Redoutensäle Wien 126
Hollein, Hans 148
Holzmanufaktur Rottweil 158, 175, 177
Hüffer/Ramin 181
Hundertmark, Hein / Cultuurhistorie
gemeente Utrecht 149
Huthmacher, Werner 122, 127

Jakobs, Dörthe 78, 79

Kaunat, Angelo 132
Klomfar+Partner 128
Kollhoff Architekten 140
Kraneburg, Christian 173

Martiradonna, Andrea 129
Marzee Gallery 117
Mazzola, Sebastiano 120
meixner-schlueter-wendt 173
Miotto, Luciana / Archivio Museo di Castelvecchio
Verona 8
Moreno, Joaquim 112
Müller, Stefan 181
Munich Technical University, Building History 113

Nemec, Studio 140

Ohara, Nobuko 123

Pavan, Vittorio 112
Prussian Palaces and Gardens Foundation Berlin-
Brandenburg 72
Prussian Palaces and Gardens Foundation Berlin-
Brandenburg, Andreas Potthoff 62
Purcell, Miller, Tritton LLP 139

Reichwald, Helmut 78, 79
Reuss, Wolfgang 79
Ricciardi, Enrico 45
Richters, Christian 109

Sánchez López, Eduardo 33
Schnieringer, Karl 55
Schubert, Leo 85, 112
Schwarz, Ulrich 140
Serrano, Manuel 117, 121
Sloun, Etienne van 125
Snower, Doug 11
Sternberg, Morley von 108
Storemyr, Per 90
Suzuki, Hisao 33

Trapp, www.tobiastrapp.eu 119
Toeten, Sybolt 152

Wett, Günther R. 145
Wicky, Gaston 131
Winde, Jörg 28
Wolf, Peter 187

Young, Nigel / Foster+Partners 154

Zecc Architekten 130
Zugmann, Gerald 156

All other illustrations have been provided by the
authors.

ON THE AUTHORS

Prof. Dr.-Ing. Johannes Cramer

Freelance architect, Professor of History of
Architecture and Urban Development

After his architectural studies, Johannes Cramer
worked at the TH Darmstadt, the DAI German
Archaeological Institute and was recipient of a
Heisenberg Scholarship at the University of
Hanover. From 1989 to 1997 he was Professor of
History of Architecture and Settlement Development at the University of Bamberg, since 1997
Professor of History of Architecture and Urban
Development at the Technical University of Berlin.
He has led research projects on buildings from
Roman times (Basilica of Maxentius, Rome) to the
20th century (Berlin Wall). He has published widely on building surveying, building research and
archaeology as well as on various architectural
topics from medieval times as well as 20th century
architecture, including World Heritage sites such
as St. Michael's Church in Hildesheim and the old
town of Istanbul.
http://baugeschichte.a.tu-berlin.de

Since 1977 Johannes Cramer runs an office for
building archaeology, building research and building conservation and is a consultant to the
UNESCO. He has undertaken restoration and conversion projects throughout Germany and Europe,
often on buildings with valuable and sensitive
building substance. These include World Heritage
sites such as St. Mary's and Imperial Cathedral in
Speyer and the Pergamon Museum in Berlin.
Furthermore, he has undertaken numerous conservation analyses and reports on historic buildings
in preparation for their correct and appropriate
historical renovation and conversion.
www.prof-cramer.de

Dr.-Ing. Stefan Breitling

Stefan Breitling studied classical archaeology in
Freiburg im Breisgau and architecture at the
Technical University of Berlin. In 1996 as part of
the Graduate College for Art History, Building
Archaeology and Conservation at the Otto Friedrich
University of Bamberg and the Technical University of Berlin, he received a doctoral scholarship
from the DFG German Research Foundation. From
1998 to 2003 he was a research associate, later an
academic associate at the chair for History of
Architecture and Urban Development at the
Technical University of Berlin with Professor
Johannes Cramer. He completed his doctoral dis-
sertation on Manor houses between the Elbe and
the Oder 1400–1600 in 2001 at the Faculty of
Architecture of the Leibniz University of Hanover
with Professor Cord Meckseper.

He has led research projects on the Ri-Rdzong
Monastery in Ladakh, on houses in Fener, Istanbul,
on the Basilica of Maxentius in Rome, the Ottonian
Collegiate Church in Walbeck, Naumburg
Cathedral, the Franciscan Cloister Church in Berlin
and other buildings. From 1999 to 2004 he was
commissioned by the Nidaros Domkirkes
Restaureringsarbeider to lead the historical investigation of the octagonal apse of Nidaros Cathedral
in Trondheim. From 2002 to 2004 he was commissioned by the ARGE Pergamon Museum to plan
the restoration and archaeological preparation of
the Mshatta Façade in the Museum for Islamic Art
in Berlin. Since 1997 he works as a freelance
architectural historian and conservation expert. He
is a member of the Koldewey Society and the
Wartburg Society for research on castles and forts.
Since 2006 he is a Visiting Professor of Building
archaeology and history of architecture at the Otto
Friedrich University of Bamberg.